ABOUT THE AUTHOR

$\mathcal{B}$orn and brought up in Hyderabad, my passion for writing has been nurtured since a tender age of 14. Graduating in literature in 2020,I primarily explored the realms of poetry until encouragement from loved ones inspired me to venture into the realm of love stories. However, this book serves as only the beginning, as I envision a future of crafting captivating mystery novels.

Drawing inspiration from a true story, I urge readers to embark on this literary journey, promising a profound reason that unveils itself at the book's heartfelt conclusion.

You can follow me on instagram @ritvik_gadhey and also my partnered page @moulded_heart.

A POSTCARD THAT WAS NOT SENT

Ritvik Gadhey

Chennai • Bangalore

CLEVER FOX PUBLISHING
Chennai, India

Published by CLEVER FOX PUBLISHING 2023
Copyright © Ritvik Gadhey 2023

All Rights Reserved.
ISBN: 978-93-56484-10-8

This book has been published with all reasonable efforts taken to make the material error-free after the consent of the author. No part of this book shall be used, reproduced in any manner whatsoever without written permission from the author, except in the case of brief quotations embodied in critical articles and reviews.

The Author of this book is solely responsible and liable for its content including but not limited to the views, representations, descriptions, statements, information, opinions and references ["Content"]. The Content of this book shall not constitute or be construed or deemed to reflect the opinion or expression of the Publisher or Editor. Neither the Publisher nor Editor endorse or approve the Content of this book or guarantee the reliability, accuracy or completeness of the Content published herein and do not make any representations or warranties of any kind, express or implied, including but not limited to the implied warranties of merchantability, fitness for a particular purpose. The Publisher and Editor shall not be liable whatsoever for any errors, omissions, whether such errors or omissions result from negligence, accident, or any other cause or claims for loss or damages of any kind, including without limitation, indirect or consequential loss or damage arising out of use, inability to use, or about the reliability, accuracy or sufficiency of the information contained in this book.

This book is dedicated to all the people out there who love unconditionally.

ACKNOWLEDGEMENTS

Thanks to my brother, Ratul Kashyap, who helped me make this book possible – He kept pushing me to bring an excellent piece out.

Thanks to Pulkit Prasad for inspiring me and having my back all the time.

Thanks to Barnisha, my project manager for the book, who has been patient in working with me.

Thanks to Rakesh Thata, who heard my ideas, gave me feedback and encouraged me.

Thanks to Arvind Vikiram KB, for encouraging me and being patient while I was developing the story.

Thanks to Srinitha Bhagoji, for reading the book and being critical so that I could make changes to the book and make it readable.

Thanks to Rohit Sai Dodla, for being blunt while I shared a part of the story and not to put it in.

Thanks to my mom, Krupa Rani Gadhey and my dad, Bhasker Rao Gadhey, for encouraging me and feeling proud of whatever I did.

Last but not the least. Thanks to Roamate Hostel and the team who gave me the perfect environment to develop the story.

CHAPTER 1

*D*river, can you please go a little bit fast? I am getting late for the flight. I said.

Flight kitte baje ki hai sir? (When is the flight?) The driver asked.

The flight is at 8:30, and it's already 7'o clock. I said.

Domestic or international? The driver asked.

Domestic. I said.

Phir toh koi tension nahi hai, aap aaram se baito mai apko 30 minutes mai paucha dunga. (Then there is no need to worry; we will reach the airport in 30 minutes. Sit back and relax!) The driver said.

But I have to get the boarding pass, and I have to be there at least 2 hours before, and I have only 1 hour left. I said.

Web check-in kar chuke ho? (Did you do the web check-in?) The driver asked.

Yes, I said.

Don't worry. One hour is enough. The driver said.

This is my first time taking a flight. I always used to take the train. I said.

No problem sab! (Sir) Stay calm! The driver said.

Okay. I said, but I was still worried.

Vaise ap ho kaha se? (Where are you from?) The driver asked.

Mai Hyderabad se hu. (I am from Hyderabad.) I said.

Oh! Mai vahi soch raha tha. (I was wondering the same.) The driver said.

Kya? (What?) I asked.

Apka slang bahut alag lag raha tha. (Your slang is different and does not sound like you are from here.) The driver said.

Acha! (Oh, okay.) I said.

The choice of words in Hindi is also not correct. The driver said.

Matlab kya hai apka? (What do you mean?) I asked.

Arey bura mat manna sab lekkin apka Hindi sahi nahi hai. (No offence, sir, your Hindi is not up to the mark.) The driver said.

Arey uncle hum Hyderabad wale mai kamiyan hai lekkin hum dil se bahut ache hai! (We, Hyderabadis, indeed have faults but are good at heart.) I said.

Acha! (Oh, okay!) The driver said.

Yes, and agar koi kamiyan hai toh b hum agar taan liye kuch karne keliye to hum woh karke dikhayenge. (Yes, and we are so determined. If we decide to do something, we will do it no matter the cost.) I said.

Acha, badiya! (Oh! Great!) The driver said.

2

Yes. Kabhi aana Hyderabad. Duniya ke sabse achi Biryani khilaunga! Yelo mera visiting card. (Yes. You should come to Hyderabad once and try our world's famous Biryani. This is my visiting card.) I said.

Waah! Aap writer ho? (Wow, are you a writer?) The driver asked.

Yes, actually, freelance content writer. Call me when you come to Hyderabad, and I will arrange accommodation. I said.

You took my words seriously. The driver said.

Indeed, I did and that resulted in our friendship. I said.

Vaise Delhi kis kaam se aaye ho? (By the way, why have you come to Delhi?) The driver asked.

Mera Hindi karab hai na, issiliye sikhne aya hu. (My Hindi is bad, right? I have come to learn it.) I said sarcastically.

Acha! Sikhliye phir? Hindi? (Oh! Did you learn it then?) The driver said sarcastically too.

Kya kare? Jisse b mila woh bewakoof nikla, including you. (What to do? Whomever I met they were all stupid, including you) I said.

What? The driver asked.

Just kidding! I said.

Okay, we have arrived at the airport. The driver said.

Thank you! I said.

We reached the Indira Gandhi International Airport in 30 minutes from the hotel I was staying, as promised by the driver. I took the boarding pass, completed the formal security check, and rushed to the flight. I was taking Air India.

A sigh of relief; finally, I boarded the flight and sat in my seat.

Hi! My name is Ritvik. I said.

Ahhh… Do I know you? The person who sat towards my right said.

No, I said.

Okay, He said and gave me a weird look.

He plugged in his headphones and began to play some music. I'm social and like to chat with anyone, but he seemed aloof. I wonder why some people are not interested in talking. I don't mean to criticise them, but even when someone else initiates a conversation, they give a strange look. Anyway, I get bored quickly and need something to keep me busy. I don't have a book to read or anything to watch online. I could download a movie, but it would drain my battery and data, and it might stop halfway because the flight might take off anytime. So I turned to the person who was sitting on my left.

Hi! My name is Ritvik, and you? I said.

Hi! I am Abhijeet. He said.

Nice name! Are you from Delhi? I asked.

No, I am from Hyderabad. He said.

Oh! You, too, are from Hyderabad! I must be lucky. Haha! I said and laughed.

Oh, nice that you are from Hyderabad. He said.

But you look more like a North Indian. I said.

Yeah, I have heard that from many people. He said.

Haha! I laughed, not knowing why exactly I laughed.

Are you going to Hyderabad? He asked.

Ahh? Yeah? Is this flight going somewhere other than Hyderabad? I said sarcastically.

Actually, this flight has two destinations. One is Hyderabad, and the other is Tirupati. He said.

Oh! I am sorry. I said.

I thought I was trying to mock him for fun, but it was a complete failure. My sarcasm is really bad. I put my head down in embarrassment.

Kind attention to the passengers; we request you put on your seat belts and prepare for take off.

I was ready and gathered all my courage. This was my first time taking a flight, and I was worried that I would not puke or get frightened. To my inner self, Okay, Ritvik, come on, you can do this. Get ready! I know this is stupid, but you must be brave. Here it comes..... Yo Spiderman! Superman! Ironman! Give me strength.

The flight took off, and I was fine. I mean, I was a little frightened. It happens to everyone, I guess, while taking a flight for the first time.

Dear passengers, we have successfully taken off. Food and beverages will be provided for you. Please relax and sit back and enjoy the services provided by Air India.

God! This was my first time taking a flight, and I was slightly scared. I said to Abhijeet while turning my head.

Oh, okay. Abhijeet said.

Hey, are you alright? I asked.

I saw him crying, and I didn't know why. I didn't notice it because I closed my eyes as I was scared.

Yeah, I am fine. Sorry! He said.

No, it's okay. Do you need some water? I asked.

No. Abhijeet said.

Okay, I said.

I didn't know what to say and kept quiet for some time.

If you don't mind, can I know why you were crying? I asked him after a few minutes.

I am a curious ass, and my extroverted nature will always be at its peak.

Some memories and the things happening right now are running in my mind So.... , I cried. He said.

What is it? Don't mind. I am just curious. I said.

It's a long story. I don't want to ruin your time. Abhijeet said.

I am very patient, and I really want to know. I am a good listener too. You wouldn't regret telling me your story. I said.

Okay….. Ahh…. Are you sure? Abhijeet asked.

Yes, I am sure as hell. Tell me. I said.

Okay, this would be very emotional. I hope I will not make you feel sad. Abhijeet said.

Whatever it is, It is fine. I am here to listen. I said.

Okay! Abhijeet said.

CHAPTER 2

*A*bhijeet *begins to narrate.*

I was born in a middle-class family. With a few small dreams and goals, I completed my 10th class and joined BiPC to become a doctor. I am still not sure why I was influenced to do that in my life, but the idea of pursuing it was because of my biology teacher while I was in my school. That decision was good because I liked what I was studying. Things were going well, but I wonder if the age or the environment that college (11th and 12th class, usually called college in Hyderabad) provides makes things worse. My journey of uncertainty started 8 years ago when I was 16 years old and when I saw the first love of my life at the bus stop where I was waiting for a RTC bus to board to reach my college. I saw this girl walking to the bus stop to board the same bus to get to college like me. I didn't know who she was, so I looked at her and turned away. Then my friend, Rahul, came to the same bus stop where he was not supposed to be because it was different from his boarding spot. I saw him a couple more times when she and her friend came to the bus stop, so I just asked him why is it like that?

Hey, Rahul! Why do I always see you at the same bus stop, and why do you keep looking at that girl? I asked.

I don't look at that girl but the girl next to her. Her name is Christina. Rahul said.

Why? I asked.

She is my girlfriend, and we always go to college together. Rahul said.

I was shocked to hear this. I did not say a word after I listened to what Rahul said and just boarded the bus.

But I was curious about the story, so I tried to ask him at lunchtime as he was from the same class.

What is your story, and how did this start? I asked.

I met Christina in my 9th standard, and I have had feelings for her since then, but I never expressed it as I am kind of introverted and found it difficult to say this to her. I had the same feeling for almost one year, and during the 10th class final exams, I got the courage to say it to her. But before I expressed this to her, she came to me on the first day of the exam, and I thought she would wish me the best of luck, but she said, "I love you". I was shocked and didn't know what to say apart from saying "I love you" back. But she ran away like she just murdered someone, and I could not say. Rahul said.

Wow! I said.

I was too curious to know what happened next. I didn't waste a second.

So what happened next? I asked.

Then I met her the next day and insisted she talk to me. I asked her why she loved me, for which she obviously couldn't answer, and I liked it, and then I finally told her that I had the same feeling for her for a long time. I said that I loved her too, and then she just smiled and ran away as if she was a deer escaping from the cheetah. Rahul said.

Hahaha!!! I laughed out loud.

I was interested in the point where he was ready to propose to her, but at the same time, when he was prepared to propose to her, she proposed to him. I mean, this is a dream come true for the boys. Isn't it?

Abhijeet asked me.

I am not sure because I never experienced this teenage love. I said.

Okay. But I was interested, though. That was all new to me. Abhijeet said.

True, I agree. Go ahead! I said

Alright so…..!

****

Abhijeet continues to narrate!

I am unsure if I was in love with the girl I saw at the bus stop that morning. I think it was the age or excitement I got after listening to their stories(Rahul's and Christina's stories). Everyone in the college had a boyfriend or girlfriend. It's not that I don't have girlfriends. I never had a different kind of feeling for them. They were just good friends. I think I just got carried away with my thoughts at that moment.

Hi Rahul! I said.

Hi Abhijeet! I didn't find you at the bus stop. I thought you were not coming to the college today. Rahul said.

No, I started early today because I woke up early. Haha! I said.

Yeah, you are so dedicated to becoming what you want to become, so you woke up earlier than usual. Rahul said.

Yeah, I wish I could have really been dedicated. I said.

Hahahaha! Rahul laughed out loud.

What's up? How's everything going between you and Christina? I asked.

Nothing much, dude. Rahul said.

Oh, why so? I asked.

What do you mean? Why so? Every day won't be memorable. Rahul said.

(Yeah, right! What a stupid question) – Inner me.

You tell me, don't you want a girlfriend? Rahul asked.

Nah! I never thought about it. I said.

Why bro! You should think of it, you look good, and you dress well. Girls would just get crazy about you. Rahul said.

They were crazy about me while I was in school, but anyways, I was not interested. I said.

You better be. You know it's tough to find girls these days; when you get an opportunity, you must grab it, dude. Rahul said.

Yeah, yeah! Bullshit! I said.

Why bullshit? Rahul asked.

What do you mean by opportunity and grabbing? It just sounds so misogynistic, dude. I said.

Well, I didn't mean it that way. Rahul said.

You know… I just… Rahul shrugged his shoulders, having no idea what to say.

If you don't have an answer, I will consider that you were trying to be a misogynist. I said.

What? Huh!!! Your problem! Rahul said,

Not that, dude. Women are already treated unwell in our society, and we must change it. If you say grab her and be an opportunist, then there is no need for us to come out and have a proper education. I said.

Understood, yar, sorry! Rahul said.

Good, no need to be sorry. Although! I find the other girl interesting. I said.

Oh! Oh! Finally, some facts are coming out. Rahul said.

Huh! You bet! I said.

Do you want me to introduce you to her? Rahul asked.

No, but what is her name? I asked.

Her name's Riya. Rahul said.

Oh, that's what her name is. – Inner me.

So, would you like to talk to her? Rahul asked.

No, I said.

CHAPTER 3

I have started to see her regularly, nothing else, just watch her board the bus, and I board the same bus because Rahul used to be there with me, and Christina used to be with her.

Days passed. I thought, why not give it a try. I thought of talking to her and proposing to her. I might have gotten carried away at that moment, but I started to admire her afterwards. The feeling began to get real. And one day….

Rahul! I said.

Yes. Rahul whispered as we were in the midst of the class.

I am in love with Riya. I said.

What? Rahul whispered again.

Yeah, I said.

Dude, are you serious? Rahul asked.

What do you think? I said, and gave me a straight look in his eyes.

Okay, we will talk during the break. Rahul said.

The class came to an end; it was lunch break now.

Dude, do you love her? Rahul asked.

Yes, I do. I said.

Woah bro! You are finally in love, huh!!! Welcome to the club. Rahul said.

What? I said.

It's just the excitement, dude. Rahul said.

Dude, I am not feeling excited. What are you excited about? I asked.

Ugh!!! Jo samajdhari padai mai dikhatha h na, woh toda life mai b dikhaya karo..... nah samaj! (The level of understanding you have in studies, you don't have over life!)

Chalo ab khana khathe h...!!! (Now, let's go and have lunch) Rahul said.

Haha!!!! I laughed out loud.

I should say I was excited too, but I don't know how to express it. I didn't find a reason to express it. We both proceeded to the cafeteria in our college to have lunch.

Hey! I forgot to ask you; does she have a boyfriend? I asked.

She had one before, but they broke up. I am unsure if she has now. Rahul said.

I stopped abruptly. I gave Rahul a furious look.

Bro, why are you looking at me like that? Rahul asked.

If she has a boyfriend, then what would happen to me? You forgot about this logic and got excited about it. You are trying to make me feel excited about having feelings for her. Rukh tujhe toh!!! (wait, you are dead in my hands!) I said.

Arey Arey! Rukh jao!!(Please wait) don't hit me. She might not have a boyfriend. Rahul said.

If she has a boyfriend, then you are dead in my hands. I said.

How will that be my mistake? Rahul asked.

It will be your mistake because of you only I saw her, and you were the one who said that I look nice, and girls would just be crazy about me. I never had the interest to think of her in the first place. I said.

Abhijeet says to me.

I was lying, actually; I indeed had the interest. Abhijeet said.

Of course! You had. I said.

What do you mean? Abhijeet asked.

Men will be men! I understand that much. I said.

Haha! Yeah! Abhijeet said.

Abhijeet continues to narrate.

Yeah, I am the one who should be blamed. But if Riya has no boyfriend, you should worship to me and treat me like a lord. Rahul said.

Enough of dreaming! Get the information. I said.

We had lunch, and the day went as usual. He promised me that he would get to know about it by tomorrow.

CHAPTER 4

I met Rahul the next day at the bus stop.

So, did you find out? I asked.

No, Christina will let me know today. Rahul said.

Okay. Are we waiting for the girls to come? I asked.

Yes. Rahul said.

Okay. I said.

Why don't you start a conversation with her? Rahul asked.

Excuse me. I said.

Christina and I will be talking, and you both will be alone. You can at least speak to her generally. You said that you flirt a lot and you can make girls laugh. I don't see that happening. Rahul said.

Excuse me. I said again.

Yeah! Don't you feel that? Rahul asked.

Shut up! I said furiously.

Fine. Rahul said.

I agree with him, though. I am the one who is interested in talking to Riya, and I am the one who is not talking to the girl. I have just told him that I am interested in her, but I have thought of it many times. I should have spoken to her and got to know her better.

They are here. Rahul said.

We got the next bus, and we reached the college. As usual, Rahul moved forward to talk to her, and Riya was behind her.

****

Hi! I am Abhijeet. I said.

Hi, I am Riya, and I know your name. She said.

Oh! I know your name too. I said.

She smiled.

So, what's up? I asked.

She shrugged her shoulders and said, "Nothing".

Argh! Why am I being bad at this? – inner me.

I stayed silent and didn't say anything. I couldn't open my mouth and was so ashamed of myself. Meanwhile, we reached the college. It is just a little bit away from the bus stop we get down. So, I just said bye to Riya, and that's it. We let Christina and Riya go, and as soon as they went, I gave that look again to Rahul.

What? Rahul asked.

You know what I am expecting to hear. I said.

Okay! Okay! I got the information you needed. She is not in any relationship or doesn't love someone. Rahul said.

A relief it gave!

I know you would do that for me, that's why you are my friend! I said funnily. I said.

Now what? Rahul said.

Now you just wait and watch! I said.

****

The next day!

Hi Riya! I said.

Hi! Riya said.

You look pretty today! I said.

Thank you! She smiled and said.

So, is this your daily routine? I asked.

What? She said.

Being pretty! I said.

Haha! Pickup line, huh? Do you think I don't get them from anyone? Riya asked.

You might get them from anyone, but I don't say this to everyone. I said.

Huh! Huh! Nice one. Riya said.

Yeah, I give as good as I get! I said.

Certainly, Riya said.

Yeah, I will talk to you in the evening. Need to go! I said.

Okay! She said.

****

Rahul and Christina used to walk to their homes almost 9 kilometres away. So, Christina asked Riya to walk with them, and as a company, I would be there so that she won't get bored while walking that far.

Dude, I have good news for you. Rahul said.

First, tell me what it is; then, I will tell you if the news interests me. I said.

Why are you such a pain in the ass all the time? Rahul asked.

Hihihi…. Shut up and tell me. I said.

We asked Riya to come with us while going back home. And we said you would accompany her so she won't get bored. Rahul said.

I smiled but was still focusing on the class.

(After the class.)

You did a good thing in your life for the first time. I said.

Yeah! Asshole! Rahul said.

****

That day in the evening.

I started to walk along with Riya, and I was vibing with her well. I asked her where her schooling was and all the critical details I needed to know, and she comfortably shared them with me. The first walk and the talk were great, and my gut started to say she was the one. We shared our Facebook IDs; she left for her home, and I, too, went for mine. I started chatting with her on Facebook. Also, we used to meet each other while going to college. I wanted to get her so badly by now. The feeling was different, and I didn't know what was wrong with me. I understood that maybe this is what being in love feels like.

We were in college, and it was time for our study hour.

Dude, I think it's time for me to propose to her. I said.

What? Rahul asked.

Yes, I think I should propose to her now. I said.

You're serious, bro? Rahul said.

No, I think I am joking. I said sarcastically.

Asshole! Rahul said.

Hahaha! That's why you should not ask stupid questions. I said.

Okay! So, tell me, I thought you were just trying to get to know her, and I thought you would still take time. Rahul said.

No, I will waste time if I still get to know her. I got to know what I needed to know, and she is a good person. I think that's what I would need to get into a relationship. I said.

Great! When are you thinking of proposing to her then? Rahul asked.

Tomorrow evening. I said.

So, Christina asked her to come with us for a walk one more time and she denied it as she was not feeling well and couldn't walk that far. I did not know this, and I was getting ready for her to come, and I even started to walk with my friend Rahul assuming that she would come with us. But Christina called Rahul and said that she would not be able to come with us and said to communicate the same with me.

She was giving me a serious yet flirtatious look. She probably understood that I was going to do something like this. I was embarrassed, and I just took the bus and went home. I was totally into that look she gave me and was smiling to myself at home. But that night, I couldn't sleep, and I felt if I proposed to her and she said no, would I be able to take that? So, I wanted to wait a little longer and develop a friendship bond before I told her those three beautiful words.

The next day was normal. Rahul was here, and I told him I decided to wait a little longer. He agreed to what I said, and we took the bus.

Hi! Riya said after we reached the college.

Hi! I said.

I could not come yesterday, and I am still not feeling okay, so we can probably walk home next week. Riya said.

Okay. I said and nodded my head.

We went to our respective classes.

Finally, the day came, and as she promised, she was walking with me, and I took some courage to know her story in the past.

So I heard that you broke up with your ex. What happened?

Huh! I see you are showing interest in knowing about me. Riya said.

Yeah, I am interested, I said.

Okay. She said.

CHAPTER 5

*W*e were in a good relationship but had to break up because he cheated on me Riya said.

Wait, what? I asked.

Yeah, we had to break up because the guy was in a relationship with me and was in a relationship with one of my friends at the same time. Riya said.

Oh! Then it was not because your parents got to know. I said.

No, actually, I told my parents after what happened, and it was impossible for me to digest that. Riya said.

I tapped on her back and said it's okay.

How did you conclude we broke up because our parents got to know? Riya asked.

Rahul told me that it was because of your parents. I said.

I didn't tell anyone because everyone would see me as a fool. After all, I couldn't understand that he was cheating me even though a few of my friends said he was cheating me. You don't mention it to anyone. Riya said.

Okay. I said.

In fact, his parents knew that he was in a relationship with me. Especially her mother, I had a good rapport with his mother. I was also sure my parents would agree because he was from U.P. I mean, he was not wholly from U.P., but his mother was a North Indian, and his father was a South Indian. Riya said.

I wondered, "Will their parents agree if she gets into a relationship with me?" But I kept that to myself. And she started to talk about her previous relationship. I was mature enough that it was better to listen to her pain because that's what people want; someone to hear them out sometimes. I understood what she said, and I wanted to be the cure for what happened to her.

It was great talking to you, and I liked it. Riya said.

I realized that we reached the point where we should go back to our homes. I didn't know how time passed so fast. It was around 6:30 P.M., and I missed two calls from home. My phone was silent, and I didn't pick up the calls.

We went to our respective homes, and on the way, I promised myself I would never do something like that to her. I started liking her more and decided to propose to her soon.

CHAPTER 6

*I*t had already been a month since I was talking to her, and I finally decided to propose to her.

We were walking from the college as we did a couple of times. Rahul and Christina were coming from the back, and they were far away from us, and I was talking to Riya.

I gathered all the courage to propose to her.

Riya, I need to tell you something. I said.

Yeah, tell me. She said.

I think I am in love with you. I said.

What? She said while she was in shock.

You heard me right. I love you. I said.

She took a pause for a minute.

Abhijeet! Riya said after a deep breath.

I just had a breakup 4 months ago, and I am not sure I am still over that person. I don't know if I can get into a new relationship with you. She said.

I understand, but that's a stepping stone to move on right With ?I said.

I already moved on, but…. She said.

Then what is the problem in getting into a relationship when you already moved on? I said.

Yes, but I cannot get into a relationship right now, and it is too difficult for us because you are South Indian, and I am a North Indian. Riya said.

These stereotypes still exist in this country, and I believe everyone might have gone through these things. - Inner me.

Yes, I agree, and I know this problem will be there, but we can still manage. You are thinking about the future, and I know it's difficult, and we will reason with your parents until they agree. I said.

No, they won't and will never say yes to this. Riya said.

Then that would have happened in the case of your previous relationship as well. His father was a South Indian too, and he was based in Hyderabad. I said.

What you said is correct, and it was in the past. When I told them about my previous relationship, my father strictly advised me to never get into any other relationship and concentrate on my career. She said.

Look, I really love you, don't ask me why but I really do, and I want to spend the rest of my life with you. I said.

I understand what you are feeling, but I am not sure If I can say yes to you ever. I like you as a person, but I will not be able to accept you. She said.

I didn't know what to say about this. I just stayed silent, and we had to return to our homes as the point of returning home had come. Tears started to roll in her eyes, and I didn't know what to say. Christina asked her what happened, but she refused to answer her. Christina was giving me an angry look. I was like, I didn't do anything.

"What happened?" Rahul asked while taking me aside.

I proposed to her. That's what happened. I said.

Then why is she crying? Rahul asked.

Dude, how would I know? She just started crying. I said.

Okay, I understand. Just go home and get some sleep. We will talk about this tomorrow. Rahul said.

But why is she crying, dude? I asked.

Just leave it and go home. Rahul said.

I didn't want her to cry like this, or else I wouldn't have proposed. I said.

It's alright! You just expressed what's in your heart and nothing else. Just go home and take care. Rahul said.

I went home and said nothing to her. I was so angry at myself that day that I made her cry. I still remember the day now and probably will never forget it.

CHAPTER 7

*T*he next day, I was waiting at the bus stop.

Hi Abhijeet! Rahul said.

Hi dude. I said.

What's up? Rahul asked.

What? I asked.

You look worried. Rahul said.

Why would I not be? After what happened yesterday, don't you think I should be? I asked seriously.

Chill out, man. You haven't done a crime by expressing your feelings. Rahul said.

But your Christina saw me as if I did something to her. I said.

Hey! Take a chill pill. He said.

I am sure she must have thought that I was harassing Riya. I said.

Just don't worry. You know what? I don't care what Christina thinks sometimes. Rahul said.

What? I asked.

Yes. Christina just overthinks sometimes. So we don't have to be worried about what she thinks. Rahul said.

If she overthinks, you have to be good enough to not let her overthink. I said.

She is not your girlfriend. She's mine. Why are you worried? Haha! He said while he laughed.

Nonsense. Anyways, you are right; not my concern. I said.

Christina and Riya arrived, and we took the next bus as usual.

After getting off the bus at the bus stop near the college, she talked to me as if nothing had happened. I was almost shocked by how she was, and I was just talking to her as if she was talking but....

Abhijeet, it's better for us to be friends and nothing else. Riya said.

Okay, I don't have a problem. I said.

Okay great! Bye. She said.

Bye. I said.

Rahul sent Christina off and came to me.

What did she say? Rahul asked.

As expected, she just said, let's be friends!

What did you say? Rahul asked.

I just said Okay. I said.

So, you are going to forget her? Rahul asked.

I never did what I said. Haha! I said.

Hahaha! Rahul laughed.

I smiled, and we both proceeded to our classes.

****

Riya and I started to talk every day since then, and I always tried to bring up this topic, but she would deny it all the time. I could not say that she ultimately did not like it; instead, she was scared of the result. But we don't always care about the outcome, right?

After a few conversations, exactly on the 12th day after I proposed to her. I was too angry with her because of the conversation she and I had last night. She was all talking about being together and showing uncertainty simultaneously. But that day, she came to me wearing all traditional clothes, and I wondered that she might have gone to a temple. We both spoke on the way to the college.

So, what did she say? I saw you both talking about something. Rahul said.

She said...... I took a break.

Yeah, what did she say, dude? He asked.

She said, yes!

He was so happy, and I was on top of the world. It was the beginning of everything. A new beginning and a new chapter of my life.

CHAPTER 8

"*I*magination should be used, not to escape reality, but to create it." - Colin Wilson.

How do you feel when what you imagined becomes your reality, and you were able to create it? It was incredible to see my dreams come true and realise that I made them happen. I was overwhelmed by the emotion I felt. It was like a surge of happiness or something like that. I was totally into her, and I enjoyed the feeling of being with her. I didn't care about the consequences or the challenges that awaited me. I felt all the love in the world. I think I loved myself more than her, for winning her over. Everything was perfect until we faced the real issues we had to deal with.

Why are you worried about that thing right now? There is a lot of time left for that, and we should be concerned about settling down. Once it is done, everything will follow. I said.

No, you don't understand what I want to say. It is difficult to convince my parents. Riya said.

So, what are you suggesting? I asked.

If we both come to an agreement and get separated now, we won't get hurt that much. Riya said.

Okay, so you don't love me, and you are just scared that something might happen in the future, and you are ready to leave me now just like that. Right?

No, I do love you…. I had to stop her from making her point and said,

Then stay with me, and we will figure this out when the time comes. Now our primary focus should be on studies and not on these topics. I said.

She agreed, but I had to keep on convincing her and keep on reassuring her from time to time. But one day……

You know, my mom and I were watching a movie called "Two States" (that was the movie that was released in 2014). I asked my mom what would happen if I brought a South Indian guy and said I wanted to marry him. Riya said.

What did your mother say? I asked.

She said you will be out of the house. Riya said.

I am terrified now, Riya. I said.

I told her I would be out of the house anyway after marriage, so what difference does it make? Riya said.

God! You really said that? I asked.

Yes, she said.

What did she say next? I asked.

She gave me an angry look, and I just smirked and got off there. Riya said

Hahaha! But what if she really won't agree? I asked.

Koi na mana lenge! She said, (We will get her to agree!)

That was the first time I ever saw a glint in her eye, and that was the first time I ever heard her say that thing confidently. Nothing is impossible. You just need the courage and the confidence to persuade them, and you will get them. When you love someone or something unconditionally, you will be willing to endure any kind of pain. Yes, people do say that you will be hurting your parents too. But I think parents also want their kids to be happy. Sometimes, parents are stubborn about getting their kids to agree to arranged marriages. Still, even in those cases, you have a choice to pick a guy or a girl. I think things are changing. It doesn't matter anyway because even after marriage, they will have to love each other to stay together.

As we approached the eighth month of our relationship, she began to have trouble breathing. She was rushed to the hospital several times, but the doctors couldn't diagnose her problem. They said she had to eat well and be strong. Everyone was so worried about her that they kept stuffing her with food.

How are you feeling now? I asked.

I am okay. Riya said.

Have you had your lunch? I asked.

Abhi toh khaya h maine aur kitna khaum? Mar jaum? (Just now, I ate. How much do you want me to eat? Probably, I will die because of eating) She shouted,

Why are you saying things like that? I asked.

We fought so much that day, and she showered all her frustration on me. I was calm because I understood she had to bring that all out onto me. The love never ended, and I could take whatever things she would say. Just to give her a little bit of relief.

It was summer, and the college was closed. It has already been 1 year and 2 months for our relationship. She still had issues with breathing in the night and restlessness. Doctors suggested visiting a psychiatrist because they concluded it was due to what she was going through in her mind. Still, her parents denied saying that she was okay. Even though she said she was fine, I knew something was wrong. I asked her many times, and she never said anything that she had any mental health issues. There was this one specific event that I had to share.

She gave me her Facebook password once and asked me to do something, I don't recall it, but I opened it. Then I saw someone texting her, and it was inappropriate, and someone was replying from her side too. I confronted her about this, and she said that her cousin had access to the account and she was texting on this side. We had a big fight over it, and when I saw her crying, I had to console her and agree with what she said. After that, I often observed her deleting messages and hiding things from me. But I kept silent because it would lead to more breaking of trust and would be more stressful for her to handle the conversation. I couldn't stop sometimes, and I used to ask her why she was deleting messages. She used to put off the conversation by saying that she had to delete the chat because her parents might use the phone sometimes, and it was true also, but it felt different. We were still fine; we went on dates and we were having a good time, but there was something that was missing.

After a couple of months.

I didn't see her for a long time because she was having many health issues already, and she was not coming to college, and I didn't feel like going to. I had an obsession with meeting her and one day, I went to meet her, and we were talking on the road. It was a casual meeting for 20 minutes, so we did not plan to go anywhere. We were talking, and suddenly, her dad came, and he saw us talking, and I had to leave immediately because she was not okay with her dad seeing us. I received a message from her saying don't text me back, and I am switching off my phone.

CHAPTER 9

I didn't know what to do, and I just waited. She turned on her mobile at night, and I received the delivery report. I texted her immediately, asking if everything was okay.

Everything was fine, but my dad said not to use the phone and give it to my mom. She replied.

God! Now will you switch off the phone again? I messaged.

Yes, She replied.

Why is there a need to switch off the phone? I replied.

No, he said that I am using the phone too much and that it distracts me. So, he instructed my mom to take away my phone after switching it off. She replied.

Okay! But how will we talk? I replied.

I will come to college, and we can talk then. Riya replied.

I was okay with that, so I didn't say anything and agreed to what she said, and then she had to switch the phone off again and give it back to her mom.

The next day was Sunday, so the college was obviously closed, and we met on Monday.

I asked, "What happened with your dad?" I asked.

Nothing happened. Riya said.

But I knew something was off, so I asked her again.

Aisa nahi ho sakta(That could not be the case), something happened, and you are not telling me. I said.

My dad kind of has doubts about me for using the phone too much, and he thinks that I am taking stress because of talking to you. She said.

What? I said.

Yeah, but nothing like that. And he just said to concentrate on my studies. Riya said.

Okay. I said.

We did not have a great talk and had to leave for classes. I was missing Riya so severely, but it was okay because I knew it would mess things up if I kept being anxious about "missing her.

Things were getting normal. It had already been a month since this happened, and her parents were normal. It was also time for our exams, which went well. We were already preparing for our competitive examinations to get good ranks and get into the fields we wanted. We decided not to go to college anymore as we planned to sit at home and prepare for the exams.

****

Hey, why don't we go to the water park? We are planning not to come to college, and it will be like a double date. Anita said.

(Anita is a friend of hers in her class. She had a boyfriend who was in the same college).

Yes, it will be a great idea. Riya said.

I am not interested in these things. It will just be a waste of time. David said. (Anita's boyfriend)

Chalo na! (let's go) It will be fun. Please! Anita said.

Yeah, it will be great. Let's go! Anyway, we are planning not to come to college. This will likely be the last time we all do something together. Riya said.

What do you say, Abhijeet? Anita asked.

I'm always in, madam! I said.

Okay. Let's go, then. David said.

Anita and Riya were excited. We planned everything and decided to leave the next day day, and it was a great day with many memories; we had great fun and took pictures together. She looked charming to my eyes that day, and I still remember that and have the sense of the feeling I had that day.

CHAPTER 10

"*R*eal maturity is when you realize that nothing is permanent" - Unknown.

But nothing is permanent, right? The next day I received a text from a stranger.

Do you know Riya? Stranger messaged.

Who is this? I replied.

Are you her boyfriend? Stranger messaged.

I was not scared of his message, so I replied, yes, I am.

Then he said she was cheating on me and in a relationship with him. I couldn't believe him, and I said that this was all nonsense and she wouldn't do something like that.

Then I immediately messaged her and asked her, "What is this all?" I didn't get a reply from her, though.

He introduced himself as Laxman, who was from U.P.

I said, Laxman, I don't believe you, and I trust her that she wouldn't do something like that with me. (Obviously through messages)

You don't believe me, right? Look at these messages. He replied.

He sent a few screenshots of their conversations. It was Riya's account, and the messages felt like hers. I will have an idea of her style or pattern of messaging right. But I still did not believe it because when we fought about the Facebook chat stuff, she said it was her cousin chatting from her profile, so I had to leave it and trust her.

These are different from what you want to prove here, Laxman. I still don't believe it, and I trust her. I replied.

He sent a picture of her on the day we went to the water park. I didn't know how he got the picture of that one because there was no way he could have gotten the image of her without her sending it to him. I started to doubt for what he was saying, and he kept sending more screenshots and more things about her, which made me think and connect the dots. Then I got a message from her.

****

My father learned about our relationship, and he is our relative whom my father instructed to talk to you in that way. And don't reply; my phone will be with my dad. She messaged.

I confronted the same with him, and he clearly said not to trust her and gave more proof that she was like that, and the dots started to make more sense to me. I knew that her father would not do something like that because he is a respectable man. He either keeps her daughter in control or just confronts me directly. He said their relationship started 4 months ago, which also made sense. All the deleting of messages and hiding things. She also said that I was torturing her, which is why she was having health issues, and I am the reason for her mental health issues. I am the kind of pervert who was behind her for favours to help put down my thirst. I couldn't believe this all, and I was utterly broken. He sent me the live messages that they were conversating during this was happening, and my mind could not take all those in, and my mind stopped working. I experienced panic attacks for the first time. I locked my room, and the anxiety was at its peak, and I was suffocating a lot, but I couldn't say this to anyone, not my parents and not to my friends or anyone. I threw my phone aside and just sat to calm myself down.

What I experienced is out of words. So, I am leaving it to you, Ritvik, to feel what I felt because almost everyone has felt these things at some point in their lives, not just a failure in love. Heartbreak is something that happens to everyone.

I understand, I said.

****

Abhijeet continues to narrate.

Two days later, I received a text from Riya.

Are you alright? Riya messaged.

I typed no.... And I wanted to confront this, but there was a point where I still believed in her. So, I again typed "Yes, I am fine" and sent it.

How is everything at home? I messaged.

It's alright now, but we can't stay together. Riya replied.

So, it's over? I replied.

Yes, I am not okay to lose you, but it has to end this way. She replied.

I don't have anything to say. Just take care and be happy. I replied.

You too, stay happy. Riya replied and blocked me.

The story of my first love ended that day. Every drop of blood, every tissue and every organ felt the pain. So many panic attacks, depression, insomnia and everything pushed every inch of my body down, trying to crush every bone. A lot of sleepless nights and a tiring life of fighting a war every fucking day to survive. No one to talk to and no one to share the pain with, all alone in a room and the pain never took a word of stopping. I started to smoke a lot. Every puff of smoke I took in was to decrease the span of life. I never stopped puff after 'puff and cigarette after cigarette' every fucking time.

Just a few days later, I had to go to college to collect certificates, and I heard someone saying, "Hey, look, the pervert is here", which I never heard from anyone. That affected me even more. I don't know who was the one who was leaking all these things, but no one is to blame here. I just stayed silent because there was nothing I could do about what others thought about me. The breakup didn't just make me depressed about what happened. But it left me alone because I could not show my face to anyone. I was digesting the truth that she cheated on me, and I have heard so many of them saying that you got cheated, including her sister once. It took a lot of energy to keep myself together. But I had to; I didn't want to, but I had to. Some family situations were going on then, and I could not collapse because it would be difficult for my parents to handle me and the problems that were going on. We moved from where we were and came to a new place. I decided never to return to that place because it would remind me of all the long walks and the conversations. A cassette of memories will play when I think of going there, and it was tough. I was starting to heal myself. The wounds were healing but left many scars on me and my character. I decided to stay silent and be a lone wolf. I could not clear the entrance exam that year and I took a gap and wanted to give it a try next year.

CHAPTER 11

They say that the love we find during our teenage years is puppy love. It sounds silly and does not feel like the real story to share. When I shared this with you, I wondered if I was in love. So, if that was not love, what was it? The pain that came from that love was real. I was depressed, and the pain of losing her was real. If that is not love, then what is it? I wanted to know the meaning of love but how?

I understood that nothing ever matters in this world. This world is poisoned with hatred and selfishness. This is the curse of the current world that we are in. "I stopped speaking because the more you say, the more meaningless you will sound." I wanted to start my life again. The way I wanted it to be. I joined coaching classes to clear the entrance examinations for the medicine course.

While I was doing that, I met this girl. She was very studious and never used to really speak that much with anyone. I liked her for the way she was. It may be because of the kind of dedication she has. But I never really gave her a chance that she could know that I think something like that of her. One day…..

Hi! Happy birthday Radha! I said.

Thank you! Radha said.

This gift is for you. I said.

What's this? Radha asked.

Check it yourself. I said,

You know, I really don't like gifts, but let me see. Radha said.

You will like it. I said.

Yeah! I love this now. Radha said.

It was a book that I gifted her. Nah! Not some textbook that I gave. It was the book "Life is what you make it" by Preeti Shenoy.

I still don't know why I gifted it to her because I need that kind of book rather than she does. I needed to change my life and have some hope for myself, but that was her birthday. I thought she could get a break from the academic books because she kept studying all day and night and needed that break to freshen herself up.

The next day.....

Hi! Can I get your number? Radha asked.

Hi! Yeah, sure. I said and gave her my number.

Just to be in touch, Radha said.

What? I asked.

I mean the number. Radha said.

Oh! Okay! I said.

I had no idea why she was feeling nervous to ask that.

Don't keep calling me daily. I said.

What? Radha asked.

You know people usually like to call me all the time. Especially the girls. I said funnily.

You are so overconfident that you think ill of girls, huh? She said.

Woah Woah! Chill out. I was just kidding. I said.

Yeah, very bad joke, huh! I am offended now. She said.

Oh, I am sorry! I didn't mean it that way. I said.

Of course, everyone says the same after they offend others. Radha said.

As I offended you, here's the chocolate. I said and gave Radha big dairy milk.

She smiled and took the chocolate.

I like dark chocolates, actually, but these work too. Radha said.

No, you read a lot, right? This helps while reading. I said.

Thank you. Radha said and blushed.

We became good friends after that. She started to give me a good vibe. I used to go to her house to study sometimes, and she was a talented girl and used to help me a lot.

Our conversations started to go endless. I was still not over the pain I was going through because of the breakup with Riya, but I had begun to feel for Radha.

CHAPTER 12

What are you doing? Don't take my picture. Radha said.

No, I want to! Shut up and smile. I said.

No… give me the phone. Radha said, and she was trying to take my phone away.

Here we go. I got the picture. Yeh!!! I said.

No… I am looking bad, and you took a picture of me. I hate you for this. Radha said.

Oh! You hate me now. Good progress. Soon you will start loving me. I said.

Don't flirt with me. You will get a hard slap on your face. Radha said.

I should have gotten by now. If I didn't get then, you must like when I am flirting. I said.

What? You mean I am characterless. Radha said while looking at me angrily.

I didn't say that. I said.

I never thought you were such a bad person. Don't talk to me. You may leave now. I don't want you in my home. Radha said.

Hey, I didn't mean that, and if you felt that way, I am sorry. I said.

Hahahahaha!!! She laughed out loud.

She was obviously joking. I knew somewhere that she must be doing this. Bluffing... Very obvious! But even I was acting. What is a man if he can't make his women laugh?

You are very innocent and compromising in nature. Radha said.

Yeah, I am very innocent. I thought you really got angry. I said.

My innocence starts when I need to impress a girl. I am good at changing colours when I need something. - Inner me.

Now, show me my picture. Radha said.

I gave her my phone.

Wow! This is really nice. Radha said.

Yes, didi. Even I liked it. Ananya said.

What are you doing here? Go to your room. Radha shouted.

Hey, why are you shouting at her? She just wanna talk, right? I asked.

She always does this. Whenever someone comes, she just barges in. Radha said.

So what? We are just talking, right? Let her be part of it. I said.

Thank you, Abhijeet. Ananya said.

Hey, call him bhaiya. He is bigger in age. Radha said.

No, that is the understanding between me and Abhijeet. What do you say? Ananya asked.

Absolutely. I said.

I am your friend, and you are taking her side. Alright! I know you will need me. Then I will show you. Radha said.

Arey!... Why? I asked.

Huh! She showed attitude.

Fine. I can't handle two ladies at a time. You go, for now, Ananya; we will talk later. I said.

Okay, all the best to convince her. Ananya said and left.

Hey girl! Natak katam karo ab.(Stop acting like a child.) I said.

Are you gonna say sorry now? Radha asked.

No way. I said.

You…!!! I will kill you. Radha said.

I don't have a problem dying. But you will be alone for life. I said.

What do you mean? Radha asked.

Ahhh??? I will tell you later. I said.

Why do you do this? Radha asked.

Arey! Let's leave the topic. I am gonna go now. I am running late, and my mom will kill me if I don't go home now. I said.

Okay, bye! Radha said.

Bye! Take care! I said.

CHAPTER 13

She called that night.

Hey! What's up? Are you not getting over my thoughts? I asked.

Enough of your flirting. Radha said.

Okay! Tell me. I said.

I was wondering. You took a good picture of mine. And I stalked your Instagram, and a few pictures that you took are excellent. And you have taken those pictures from the phone. They are really good. Radha said.

Oh! You stalked my profile. Are you interested in me or what? I asked in a flirtatious way.

Abhijeet! I told you right. Enough of flirting! Radha said.

Okay, sorry! Now I won't say anything. I said.

Yeah! I have observed you while studying. Your attention span needs to be improved, and this will not work for you. You have to be very focused when you study medicine. I am sure you will crack the exams. You are talented, and what I learn in 14 hours, you will grab within 6 to 7 hours, and that too, taking more breaks in between. But I looked at you while reading these, and I see you are not interested in cracking it. If you don't want it, then why are you struggling? I saw those pictures you posted on Instagram, and they are worth enough to say that you can become a professional photographer. Why don't you pursue it? Radha asked.

Photography is my passion, and I never considered it a profession. I said.

You should think of it or think of an alternative when you don't like this, then pursue something else for your career-wise. Radha said.

Yeah, I agree. I have lost interest in studying because of the gap that I took. I will think about it. I said.

Good! Okay, listen. I wanted to tell you this, that's why I called you. Now I have to cut the call. I will text you instead. If my mom sees me talking at this hour, she will kill me. Radha said.

Okay, good night! I said and cut the call.

I received a text from her. 'Good night and sorry! We will talk tomorrow.

She was a good person, and she thought of everyone. I wondered if someone like her would come into my life, my life would be good. I thought and decided that she would make a perfect partner.

****

One day, I expressed my feelings, and she did not say yes immediately, but she did say later. I felt my new journey had begun, and I was ready to embrace this one!

We both tried to get a good rank so that we could crack the entrance exams, but we couldn't do it. Radha got a better rank, but getting a seat was impossible because she needed to achieve more to get a seat in Open Category. She promised herself and her parents that she would do better next year. I understood by now that I had lost interest in medicine, and I thought I would give up the dream of pursuing it.

I took admission for a B.A. course and also considered Radha's advice to pursue my passion for photography. I still saw photography as a passion and not as a profession. But it is good to have something in your life. I started to focus on my career as she did.

****

Phone rings....

Hello! Radha said.

Hi! I got the admission, and my college will start in the next 5 days. I said.

That's great! But I miss you. Visit me before college starts. I wonder if we will get a chance after that. I am taking up a Pharmacy course so that my studies will continue and at the same time I can study for the entrance exams next year. If that happens, I am not sure I can meet you. Radha said.

I miss you too! I would come for sure. I said.

As planned, I went to see her at her home. I had lunch at their house and spoke with her about a lot of stuff. She said that she would not be able to meet me after this because things would get hectic for her. I understood but not that much. I mean, who would not want to meet his girlfriend, after all? We would risk it or do something stupid, but we will surely meet the love of our life.

I visited her house several times, but it started to feel different. I don't know if their parents were angry with her or me. I heard a few things that a boyfriend would not hear about his girl. Of course, she is not entirely mine, but it felt different. Her parents complained that she is not concentrating on her studies like she used to. And it somehow felt that it was because of me. After I got that vibe, I stopped going to her home.

She started to miss me, and as much as it did, I also missed her. We only had a little time to talk on the phone daily because after going home, I just got tired because of the college and the photography class I joined. I also had to study a lot, so I usually put my distractions away while I study or work.

CHAPTER 14

So, how is your photography course going? Radha asked.

It's going well. I am learning new things. I said.

Have you bought the camera already? She asked.

No, not as of now. But my brother promised that he would get one for me. Not too professional camera but a beginner-level. I said.

Whatever is fine until it gets your job done. Radha said.

Yeah, there are actually many types of cameras… I said while Radha interrupted.

Wait, hold that thought. I like to hear that, but I don't know much about cameras and will have a dumb look. I don't want to do that. Keep it to yourself. Radha said.

How rude! I said.

Arey! I am not rude. I believe in you, and you will move mountains when interested. So I don't have to hear it. Radha said.

Of course. I smirked.

Come closer. Radha said.

I moved closer, and she kissed my forehead. I kept my eyes closed when she was kissing my forehead as I felt the sense of her love passing all the way down to my toes through my veins. I could feel my heart pumping blood.

That night I couldn't sleep and could not stop my thoughts from flowing. She always says that she is not beautiful and I am much more handsome for her to handle. But after what happened that day, It was just "The world might have been ignorant in looking at this beautiful lady here. But, you must have lost your way while you were on the way to heaven and came to me. I flirt too much, you say, and I might just be exaggerating that you are from heaven. If not from heaven, maybe the architect who made you might be a perfectionist."

****

A couple of weeks later, She called me.

Do you remember to call me at least? Radha asked.

Oh, baby! How can I remember you when I didn't forget you in the first place? I said in a very flirtatious tone.

You… Don't you get tired? Radha asked.

From what? I asked.

From the flirting that you do every time? Radha said.

Nah Nah!! Never. When I flirt with other girls, I might get tired. I said.

Oh, so you are trying to flirt with other girls. This is what you are doing by going to college. Radha said.

Ahhh… No, not at all, baby! You know, right, my charm doesn't work these days. I said.

Enough! I know you. You can't live without attracting people around you. You get a lot more attention than usual. Radha said.

Ahh… No comments! I said.

Haha! Idiot. Just be careful and don't trust people too much. Radha said.

Blah, Blah, Blah!!! I said.

You never listen to me, right? Radha asked.

Wow! You got me, finally. Haha! I said and laughed.

Idiot! Radha said.

Thank you, my lady! I said.

Acha, listen! When are you coming to meet me? Radha asked.

I am not sure. And I can't come to your home. I just don't feel right. I said.

Hmm… Right. Radha said.

Do you miss me? I asked.

No, nothing like that. I was just asking. Radha said.

But I know she is missing me and needs me terribly.

I understand. I will let you know. Let's try to meet somewhere out. I said.

I don't know any place. You know, right? I usually don't step out of my home. Radha said.

Arey! I mean you are anyway joining a pharmaceuticals course. College might be starting, and we will meet there. I said.

It starts after a week. Are you saying that I need to wait till then? Radha asked.

I guess you should. I said.

Hmm… Okay. Radha said.

Don't be sad. It's just a week away, right? We will meet. I said.

Hmm… Radha sighed.

This is the powerful weapon that every woman in this world has. Whatever we say is to cheer them up, but they don't get cheered. They just say Hmm… or Okay. That is it, and then comes an awkward silence, and we don't know what to say next.

Ahh… okay, I will call you later. I am going home right now. I said.

Okay. Radha said, and I cut the call.

CHAPTER 15

After a week, I went to meet her, and I wanted to surprise her, so I did not say I was coming to see her.

I was standing near her college and waiting for her to come out. The college was already over, and she was not coming yet. I was scared she might have left or not come to college. Then I saw one of our mutual friends passing by.

Hey Swapna! I said.

Hey Abhijeet, how come you are here? Swapna asked.

I could not tell her I was here for Radha as she was uncomfortable letting everyone know. So I said...

I came to meet my girlfriend, but she still needs to come. I said.

Yes, I said I have a girlfriend. I know she could have known that Radha could be that one. But her cognitive abilities are limited, and no one would believe me if I were dating Radha. Because she was a studious person and little they could imagine that she could make me her boyfriend.

What? Do you have a girlfriend? Swapna asked.

What makes you think I can't have one? I asked.

I was wondering who must be your girlfriend. Swapna said.

You will know when the time comes. I said.

I would be glad. Swapna said.

By the way, Radha is from the same college, right? I asked.

Yes, she is talking with the lecturers. We have orientation today, so she has started to show her charm. Swapna said.

People envy her intelligence, and I do too sometimes, but she is mine, right, so if she has it, I have it too. Haha! - Inner me.

Okay. Are you leaving? I asked.

Yeah, almost everyone left. Only seniors and some juniors are left, whom I don't know. Swapna said.

Oh, okay, I will leave too in the next 15 minutes. I have some work to do. I said.

You were about to meet your girlfriend, right? Swapna asked.

No, not a problem, I can meet her some other time. I said.

At Least meet Radha. You have come this far. Swapna said.

Huh, maybe some other time. I have seen you; my heart is filled with happiness now. I said.

She smiled and didn't say anything. And I thought that little she knew that I had come to meet Radha in the first place.

Do you want to come with me? I am going back home in the same way that you will go in. Swapna said.

I might lose my mind looking at you all the time on the way back and I wont be able to remember the way to my home. I said.

No problem, you can stay at my home. Swapna said.

Haha! Don't your parents have a problem? I asked.

I live alone now. Swapna said.

Ah…. but my parents have a problem with me not returning home so… I said.

Okay, but come some other time for sure. Swapna said.

Yeah sure. Bye. I said.

Bye. Swapna said and left.

CHAPTER 16

It would not be viable to wait in vain. So I called Radha.

Where are you? I asked

In college. Radha said.

I am waiting outside your college. I said.

What? Seriously? Radha asked.

Come and see for yourself. I said.

I am coming. She said and cut the call.

She came running towards me.

What? Radha said.

I thought you would hug me, so I kept my arms open. I said.

Shut up, Idiot. Radha said.

Haha! Should I hug you instead? I asked.

No… Let's go! Radha said.

Where? I asked.

Arey! Shut up and come with me. Radha said.

She took my hand and took me to a bakery where we could sit and talk.

Is the place fine? Radha asked.

It is good, but it's outdoors. I am not sure. The dust from the road might spoil the food. I said.

So where do we go? Radha asked.

Leave it to me. I said.

I looked around and found a restaurant which serves Mandi.

I am a vegetarian, right? Radha said.

I know, but I want to eat Chicken Mandi. I said.

Oh! Okay. I will just sit with you. You eat. Radha said.

Yeah, thank you. Let's go. I said.

She moved forward and went in. I stood there and watched her while she was going. She turned around and saw me standing there, and I was smiling. She came back running.

What? Why are you not coming in? Radha asked.

What do you think? I will keep you hungry and eat in front of you? I asked.

Ahh… I can't eat non-vegetarian food. Radha said.

Stupid, look up. I said.

Sri Raghavendra restaurant, Pure veg. She read the restaurant's name out.

She looked at me and smiled.

But we have to take the stairs. It's on the 2nd floor. I said.

No problem. Radha said.

But I have. I said.

What? Radha asked.

There is one condition. I said.

What? Radha asked.

You must carry me to the restaurant or let me carry you. If that is okay, then we go, or we can go home. I said.

No. I am hungry. I can't do this right now. Cut the crap, and let's go. Radha said.

No. We have to do this. So what is it gonna be? I asked.

Okay. Let's not go. I am leaving. Radha said.

I grabbed her hand, pulled her towards me, lifted her, and took her in my arms. She was saying no, no and no. But I didn't listen. I took her up. She said no at first, but as soon as I started climbing the stairs, she shut her mouth and started to look into my eyes. At that moment, it felt that time had stopped for us to exchange some feelings. It was a beautiful moment and the most profound thing in our relationship. When we reached the restaurant entrance, I put her down, and she got reddened and blushed like anything. That face of hers said how much she loved me.

We had our lunch.

So, when are you planning on leaving me? Radha asked.

What do you mean? I asked.

You might have found someone interesting in your college. Radha said.

Yeah, I am some womaniser, right? I will date all of them at once. I said angrily.

Hey! Calm down! I am sorry. I was just joking. Radha said.

I was angry, but I couldn't hold my tears because of the label that I got when there was no mistake of mine after the break up with Riya. I still don't know how to explain how I felt because of that false labelling that I got. All those thoughts made me weak. I didn't want to blame anyone, but I was suffering. That is why I talk to people funnily and try to be friendly so that I have people around me. I have started doing this only after meeting Radha because she is the hope that I got. I still maintained no connections with my 11th and 12th mates because what they will do is just amplify the sadness I had because of that phase in my life. I have tried to make new connections so that those new connections keep me busy and help me grow out of the pain. A label of 'pervert' at that vulnerable age was something I could not handle, and I wish no one had to go through that pain.

What happened, Abhijeet? Tell me now. You never tell me anything. Open up now. Radha said.

I told her what I went through, and she became that shoulder which I needed to lay on and get relief from the suffering. She promised that she would never say something like that again. I am a ideal person and I might behave like I am not but I know I am and the people who are closer to me know that.

We both talked for some more time and then left.

****

I wanted her to be happy. But all the time, she was worried that she would be unable to do what she wanted. She was putting that effort into making her parents proud, but she was draining herself from within, and watching her do this was much harder for me.

The timings of my college and her college were odd. My house was under construction when we were in a relationship, and I was the only one to help my dad. After returning home from college, I was busy helping my parents. Not that much of a help but my part of it.

She used to miss me so much. No matter what, I was her relief from the stress that she was in. I decided that whatever it took, I would visit her at least once or twice a month, not at her place but at her college.

My college used to get over at 3:30 PM, and her college used to get over at 5:30 PM. Her college was 25 km away from my college. At this point, I used to take a bus to my home first and then from my house, I used to take a bus to her college. And by the time I reach her college. It will be 6 PM. We used to get significantly less time than we thought we would get because she must travel the same distance to get back to her home. But honestly, that very little time we had would mean a lot to her, and she used to feel happy. No matter what, she never complained about anything.

I used to get stressed entirely when I returned home after meeting her. Once I got home, my dad and I used to get some things needed for the construction to continue the next day. But still, it was okay for me. At the end of the day, we all do things to stay happy.

CHAPTER 17

You are ignoring me these days. You have no time for me. I have asked you to come to my home to meet as you are facing trouble to travel that long, but you still don't, how many times ever I tell you to come. Radha said.

Radha, understand this. You might think your parents will understand and won't say anything, but they will only see me as a disturbance. I said.

No, they all like you very much. You can talk to me peacefully, and I can also talk to you very peacefully. Radha said.

No, Radha, you do not understand my point. They might think wrong about you and me, and I don't want that to happen. I said.

Nothing like that would happen. Radha said.

No, I won't come to your home. I am not comfortable. I said.

You are stubborn. Radha said.

Yes, I am stubborn. What are you going to do? I asked in anger.

You won't understand. Radha said.

I hung up the call and didn't say anything after that. After Radha did not clear the entrance test, whenever I went to her home, I could sense that I should not be present there. I tried to avoid those situations. That is the reason I have stopped going to her home. I wanted to make her understand but girls! We can never conquer them in any arguments, right? Abhijeet asked.

True. I said.

Yeah anyways. Abhijeet said and started to narrate the story.

Finally, I agreed and went to her home once.

I was arrogant then because she finally lured me to come to her home. I was talking like I didn't care, but I do care.

You know what? I have failed my parents by not clearing that exam. Radha said.

Nothing like that. You have the potential to crack the exams, and I know it. Don't stress yourself too much about this. I said.

I will concentrate on this and get the seat next year and make them feel proud. Radha said.

You better do that. And I will not at all disturb you from now. I will not at all call you or text you. I said.

Shut up. Don't do such a thing and make me sad. Radha said.

No! That is what I would like to do right! I want to irritate you. I will torture you. Haha! I am a monster. I said.

Yeah! Your acting skills could be better. Don't ever try that again. Radha said.

Don't you dare challenge me? You were the one who fell for me. If I had not flirted with you, we wouldn't be talking. I said.

Shut up! I fell for you as a person, not because you flirted with me. Idiot! She said.

I was just joking! Cool. I said.

No matter what, when someone likes us for who we are they stay for a long-long period.

Many fights happened between me and her, but we never got separated except for……

I hate you. I said.

Abhijeet, what's wrong? I will never ask you to do anything. Just stay! She said while crying.

No, we will have to break up. I am done with this relationship. I said.

We will sort things out. Please don't leave me. Radha said.

No, the more I am with you, the more you become obsessed with me. This must end. I said.

No Abhijeet. Please, let's not do this. She said.

I want to end this, and I am willing to do it. I said, and I cut the call.

****

She called me several times, but I did not pick up the calls, and then I received a call from her mother.

Abhijeet! Hi.

Hi Aunty!

What happened between you both? Her mother asked.

Nothing happened. Everything's fine! I said.

No, I see nothing is fine, and I have observed something is wrong. She said.

Aunty, I promise you nothing is wrong. I said.

She doesn't concentrate as she used to. This has been happening ever since you have come into her life. My daughter was never like this. Abhijeet, listen to this carefully. If you both get successful in your lives, I will talk to her father and will have you people married. She said.

Hmm.... Okay, Aunty. I said.

Yeah! From now don't call her and focus on your life, and she will focus on her life. Be successful and come back. She said and cut the call.

I didn't know what had just happened, and I was shocked by the phone call from her mother. I didn't get a call from her that day.

****

The next day she called me when she was in college, and I lifted the call.

Tell me. I said.

Abhijeet, what's wrong with you? Let's not do this, please! Radha said.

I kept quiet.

I love you so much that I can't imagine my life without you. Radha said.

I don't want to leave you too. I said.

Then, why? Why are you doing this? You never tell me what happens in your life and what you think. How will I ever know? Radha asked.

I kept quiet.

Talk now, at least! Radha shouted and started to cry.

My parents learned that we were in a relationship, and they didn't like it. That's why I am breaking up with you. I said.

This time she kept quiet.

And your parents also got to know. Your mom called me yesterday. I said.

What? She said.

Yes, your mom called me. Don't you know? I asked.

No, she didn't say anything to me. I was at home all day, and she was with me. Radha said.

No, you are lying. Something happened. I said.

Trust me, Abhijeet! Nothing happened. Radha said.

Then why did she call me? I asked.

I don't know! She said in a loud voice.

She told me you are not concentrating on your career and studies as before. I said.

Radha kept quiet.

She said if we focus on our lives and become what we want to become, she will agree to get us married. If she said that, she knew we were in a relationship. I said.

Abhijeet! Listen, she doesn't know anything and if she said that to you, she likes you so much. That is why she said what she said. Understand this, she would never talk softly. She will speak so harshly that you cannot reply to her. I have never seen my mom that soft. She was never like that with me, but if she is with you, then you are the man. Radha said.

I kept quiet.

Abhijeet? She said.

Yes, tell me. I said.

I love you so much, and I want you in my life. Radha said.

I love you too! I am sorry. I will do what I can do. But we will have to talk less than before. I can't meet you like I did before. I said.

Anything is fine! I will bear the pain of not talking to you, but I don't want to lose you. Radha said.

I love you so much! I said.

Me too! She said.

Okay, listen, I must cut the call because my dad and I are going out. I said.

Okay! Okay! Take care. Radha said.

You too, take care! I said and cut the call.

CHAPTER 18

I understood that things would be different from now on, and it will be complicated for her. You know the cost of freedom is always high and tough to find. She was tied to me, and she always lived in my thoughts. I have seen her multiple times that she was distracted because of me.

Radha! I texted.

Yes, tell me. Radha replied.

This is not working out, and we need to break up. I replied.

Abhijeet, no, please!

I am sorry, I can't handle the pressure from my parents. Please, let's end this. I texted.

Please! No! No! No! She replied.

I will miss you and goodbye! I replied.

I ended it! I ended it in a horrible way that it would break her heart. I know that this was very bad.

The reality is…

I understood from her behaviour that she was obsessed with me, which could be bad for her. I always wanted something good to happen to her.

Whenever I used to go meet her, there was a sense of dissatisfaction that she could not do what she wanted, and she sometimes complained that she felt alone when she was with her parents. The worst feeling you will ever have is feeling alone, even when people are around. I didn't want to make her feel alone, but I could not do that. Though she never complained that she felt alone with me. I know I was not giving her enough time.

"The most challenging choices that we make in our life require the strongest will."

The reality is that my parents never got to know that we were in a relationship. I lied to her that they got to know. As much as I lied to her, I also lied to myself that I was perfect for her. I wanted her to grow and achieve what she wanted, and she was determined to do it. She always said that what is happening with you will never influence my life, and she is not too weak for things to come between me and her. But how much ever you try, things will affect you at least a bit. I think that's what was happening to her. That is the reason I wanted to break up with her and move ahead. This will enable her to do something in life, and I may also do something. Freedom costs you more than anything. I wanted to free her and myself, too, so that I would not have to regret that I was the reason for her failure.

But leaving her cost me more than I thought. She was a shield that protected me from feeling lonely. I was having a bad time in college because of the toxic people and fake friends around me. I couldn't get a friend to talk and share my emotions properly. When I was in that situation, she was the one I had to talk to. But now, I don't have her anymore, and the arrows that the armour was taking hit me and put me down.

That's when I decided not to let anyone come near me. I became cruel as the lord of hell would be. I always missed her, but then I bought a bike, thanks to my mom and dad, who helped me get it. After getting the bike, I started to travel by bike. Though my parents didn't like it, they could never stop me. It gave me relief from the pain I was going through. I never told my mom and dad that this is why I am doing this. The irony is that travelling on a bike is very painful; your butt will ache like anything after 200 km, and you would want to stop, but I was getting relief from the pain I already was going through whenever I rode. It was curing the wounds that I got from the breakup with Radha.

CHAPTER 19

After breaking up with Radha, two years later, I liked a girl in college and expressed my feelings to her. Her name was Keerthi. She didn't accept me, but she was in touch with one of my friends from my college. She told him I was uncertain and had an unstable mentality, so she did not accept me. When I heard that, I smirked and asked myself, how will I not be? After Riya left, the hole left in me was not filled, and I was always searching for love. I found Radha, but things could not work out with her too.

I received a call from Rahul after a couple of weeks.

Hi, Abhijeet! Rahul said.

Hi Rahul! How are you? Long time no see? I asked.

I am fine, dude. And indeed a long time, because you are the one who turned ghost after our college. Rahul said.

What can I say? I am the ghost of Uchiha. Haha! I said and laughed.

Huh? I don't know what you said. Rahul said.

You never disappointed me, Rahul. You are dumb, as always. I said.

You, too, have never disappointed me, Abhijeet. You are an asshole, as always! Rahul said.

Haha! For you, indeed I am. I said.

Hahaha! Where are you now? I think we should meet. Rahul said.

Yeah, I will meet you tomorrow. I said.

Sure! See ya! Rahul said.

Yeah, sure. Bye! I said.

Bye!

****

As I said, I went to meet him.

Hey, my man! Mota hogaya re tu!(You have become fat). Rahul said.

I didn't become fat. You have become thinner. I said.

Tera self-obsessed behavior shayad kabhi chutega nahi! (You will never lose the self-obsession that you have for yourself). Rahul said.

You bet! I said.

So have you found any new girlfriend after Riya? Rahul asked.

Yeah, I did. But you know things did not work out. I said.

Oh! What happened? Rahul asked.

Huh! It's a long story. I will tell you some other time. You tell me, what's up with Christina? I asked.

I wanted to meet you for that itself. We are not on talking terms now. Rahul said.

What the fuck happened? I asked.

Her parents and my parents came to know about our relationship, and she was forced to leave me, and even my parents restricted me a lot. This happened a while ago, but I couldn't tell you this because my father broke my phone, so I lost your contact number. Rahul said.

How sad. I am sorry, dude. I said.

Can you help me get in touch with her? Rahul asked.

How can I help you? I asked.

Can you get in touch with Riya and get her to contact Christina? Rahul asked.

Really Rahul! You know what I went through, and you still ask me for a favour? I said.

I know I am sorry, but I really want Christina. Rahul said.

Dude, listen, I think she moved on. Because it has been a while, and she has not contacted you yet. If that is the case, it's not just because of their parents. Christina isn't a small kid; she can contact you whenever possible. I feel that you shouldn't spoil her life by contacting her. I said.

I know, but I want her. Rahul said.

Rahul! Understand this, you can't get her back. What you will do is just ruin her life and yours. I said.

Just the way you ruined Riya's life, right! Rahul said.

What do you mean? I asked.

I heard those rumours. Everyone was talking about you. You might have tried to force Riya. Rahul said.

That's it! Enough of your nonsense! I said and punched him in the face, for which he fell.

One more word from that mouth, and you are dead! I said.

I am sorry! Rahul screamed.

Sorry about my foot! I never expected you would say the same. You were my best friend, and you were with me from the beginning till the end. And you have the audacity to say such a thing. I said.

I know. I am sorry. I am frustrated; that is why I have said that. Rahul said.

There is no excuse for what you said; what you just have to do is to move on. Find someone and never bother to call me again. Goodbye! I said.

Did you move on? Rahul asked while he was still down.

What? I asked.

Did you get over the feeling that you had for Riya? Rahul asked again.

Yes, I did. I said.

No, you didn't. Why do you think you could not be in a relationship with your new girlfriend? It's because you did not move on after you broke up with Riya. Rahul said.

Go home, Rahul! I said and turned away from him.

I started the bike, sat on it, and returned home. When I was heading back, I thought, is it really like that? Am I still not over Riya? I am still determining. I wondered if it was better that Keerthi did not accept me, or else I might have ruined her life too. What Rahul said could have been true because I don't give up so easily. I find solutions even when there is a 0.01% chance that things could work out. But I did give up on Radha. So why did I do that? Those things started to run in my mind. I loved Radha so much. What she did for me and how I changed after that is a part of my life which is worth than anything else.

CHAPTER 20

I might have moved on because it was already four years since I broke up with Riya now. But it really got me thinking. Was I true to myself that I left Radha for her good? Why haven't I tried to work around some other solutions? I felt pathetic. I wanted to change that, and I have tried to change myself. But, I can't return to Radha now and say, I realised and achieved enlightenment. I need to change myself. Both mentally and physically. I have to start questioning myself and find answers to them. I have to embrace my own self. I joined the gym, and I got a job after my graduation. And things were going well.

One day I met a girl who was from my office. It was the time when CoVid-19 was at its peak, and we all were working from home. So how did I meet her? Hahaha! It was in the Zoom meetings. There was nothing special about her; it was pretty much the same. But I felt like starting a new life. She felt the same.

The Magic in new beginnings is truly the most powerful of them all - Josiyah Martin.

Love, it's a magical feeling which is most potent in this universe, and a man's love is limitless and unconditional. She was not the most beautiful, but the only one I could see. When you love someone, you can move mountains for them. The strength is the same, whether a girl or a boy. But.......... Do we choose the wrong people, or are they all bad? The first three months were beautiful. The most beautiful feeling I had after a long time. I didn't want to lose this one. I was not ready for something like that.

"It is not the person we are with. It's the feeling we have with that person which makes it the most precious one." - Ritvik Gadhey.

I have been waiting to meet you. Sanjana said.

Oh, you were waiting to meet me, Sanjana! This is something new. I said.

Shut up, Abhijeet. Now give me your shoulder. She said.

Shutting up is not in my blood. I said.

She laid on my shoulder and said nothing, and I just had to keep quiet. I sensed something was off, so I had to shut my mouth this time.

I don't want to work today. I want some peace. It would be good if we didn't have to go to work today. Sanjana said, still lying on my shoulder.

We can do that because you know we didn't swipe in, so there won't be a record that we came to the office today. I said.

Are you suggesting bunking the office? Sanjana asked.

What else would I be suggesting? I asked.

I don't want to lose my job, so it's a NO. She said.

I am risking my job as well. Do you realize that? I asked.

Yes, that's why it's a double NO. She said.

Hahahaha! I laughed.

But we can go out for some time, relax, and then return. We will just say some reason for being late to work. Sanjana said.

I was waiting for something like this. Let's go! I said.

I took my Royal Enfield Thunderbird out, which is obviously a therapy for my life. It's a white colour thunderbird which looks like a wolf in the winter, and its rage is like a flaming sword made of metal. Okay………. Why am I saying this? He said.

It's okay; you can feel a little excited about the bike that you have, I said.

Thanks for understanding, Ritvik. He said.

Let's get back to the story now. I said.

Abhijeet continues to narrate.

Okay, we only went for a short ride. It was just for a quick spin but lasted for a long time.

I am happy that I am doing this with you. I never tried or thought of bunking college, but I am here with you bunking office. Sanjana said.

You know we are not technically bunking. You were the one who said NO……! Remember? I said sarcastically.

Huh! Enough of gaslighting. Sanjana said.

Oh, me and gaslighting? Did we exchange our characters or what? I said.

Shut up! Acha, listen na… I don't want this night to end. Sanjana said.

Then let's bunk the office! Nothing will happen; we will manage. I said.

Are you sure? Sanjana asked.

Yes, I'm damn sure. I said.

Okay…. Sanjana said.

Finally, as I said, it did not just last for sometime. It lasted all night. We both received a call from our team leader. She said she had a health issue but was questioned about taking an office cab. I came on my bike, so there was no record of me coming to the office that day, and I said that I left the bike in the office and took an Ola to drop her at home. And I gave a reason that she is a woman, and it is unsafe for her to go to her home alone. Who would look in so much detail for my bike that it was present in the cellar of the office? There are so many bikes, and no one knows my registration. The tool was not working, and my team leader did not question me as much as he did her. But the risk was worth it.

At least that was the only good memory that I had with her. Abhijeet said.

Huh Huh! Good memory, what did you do? I said.

Stop thinking, you are wicked-minded. Nothing happened; we just chilled. Abhijeet said.

Okay, now I will not interrupt you from narrating until you finish.

Abhijeet nodded!

Abhijeet takes over the narration.

We talked so much, or should I say I listened to her, whatever she said. Haha! It's all the same; we all men have this full-time job of listening to our partner for which we don't get paid. And there are so many things for which women don't get paid. Let's not get into that.

Hey Abhijeet, I wanted to tell you something which I shared with only a couple of people. Sanjana said.

Yeah sure. Let me get you ice cream, and then we'll talk. I said.

She sat down, depressed, and I went to get the ice cream. I was looking at her but did not realize what was happening.

Here, have it and tell me. I said.

She took the ice cream.

I asked her, "What happened?"

I wanted to share an incident that happened to me; I never said to anyone, but I feel safe sharing this with you. Even a couple of people who know this don't know the details of it. I trust that you will understand. She said.

Listening to her tone, I understood this was serious, and I was prepared for whatever she said.

At the age of 9, I was raped and tortured by my cousin's brother. He took me that day, saying he would make me study and play with me sometime. But he played with me inappropriately, in a way that would break me and leave a scar on my life that I could never get rid of. I was so small and didn't know what was happening, but I understood I was being abused. He shut my mouth with his hand, behaved like an animal and treated me like I was some machine that had no feelings. I cried, shouted, and tried to fight but was too weak to do it all simultaneously. He said, "Nothing would happen, and it is okay". It is not Okay. It is not. Not for one time, but he did this with me a lot of times, almost every day. I was too scared to say this to my parents.

I tried, but they never heard me. Sometimes, I used to play outside with my other fellow friends, and he would call me to his house, seeing a time when no one would be, and he would rape me again. I never used to agree to go to his house, but he would force me. I said several times to my mom that I didn't want to go, and he was bad, and she never understood and never realized why I was saying that. He continuously tried to touch me inappropriately in front of others. Just as I was young and a kid, everyone thought nothing was wrong with it. He did this for four years, and when I went through puberty, my parents started to be careful. Why don't the parents get to their senses before that? In those four years, he tried to get to me so many times, I didn't go several times, but sometimes my mom used to shout at me for the behaviour. I sometimes felt that my mom sent me, knowing I was getting abused.

She started to cry, and I hugged her and said nothing. I just consoled her, and she cried a lot that night, and my T-shirt got wet because of her tears.

Nothing ever goes as planned in this accursed world. The longer you live, the more you realize that the only things that truly exist in this reality are merely pain, suffering and futility. - Madara Uchiha.

That was the one and last meaningful conversation with her, and after that, everything was just a dream.

****

You always had a problem with whatever I did. Sanjana said.

No, I never did. Whatever you did is okay for me. I said.

No, you all are the same; no one understands me. Not my father, not my mother and now you are also doing that. She said.

Arey… understanding is what I have been doing since we were in a relationship. That is what I was trying to do, and that is what I will be doing. I said.

Huh…you? You understand shit. You don't have the mindset of understanding things. You don't have clarity on your own life. You have not even understood what you want in life. You are working in a company, and you want to study UPSC, and you also want to have a business. You are a pool of uncertainty. She said.

I am working right now for myself so that when I don't have a job, I can concentrate on my studies as I will have my own savings and don't have to depend on anyone. I want to crack UPSC, but I also want to own a small business. Why can't a person have multiple interests? I asked.

It does not work like that. Sanjana said.

Why not? Let me explain to you. Even if I set up a business before I further study for UPSC. I will gain some experience, which will be like a pet project. When I sit in front of the interviewers, I will have more things to add to my CV. If the business runs nicely, I will automatically create an impression that even if I have a successful business, I want to come into service. That will make them feel that I am genuine and will work dedicatedly. I said.

You…..! I am not even sure that you will crack it. It's better for you to forget me. Sanjana said.

Tears just rolled from my eyes, and I couldn't imagine she would say something like that.

She just cut the call after saying that. I cried a lot after that. There was no chance that I could show my tears to anyone. Because there is this stereotype that men shouldn't cry. I never wanted to show my pain to anyone because that would just amplify the pain that I was in. What would have happened if I had expressed what I was going through? They listened to the story and did what? Nothing! Right?

I just convinced myself that everything would be okay and smiled.

She called me after some time.

Hello, tell me. Sanjana said.

What should I say? I said.

Okay, there is nothing to say, right? Bye then. She said and cut the call again.

It made me sad. I mean, what are you trying to do? I put my self-respect aside and talked to her, no matter how much she hurt or was disrespectful. I listen to her all the fucking time, and then what I get is mistreated.

She called me again.

What are you doing? She asked.

Nothing. I said.

What are you trying to hide? She asked.

I instantly cried because it was tough to hold those tears.

Uff…..! Why are you crying like a small child? Oh sorry! I forgot this is what you do, act like crying and make me feel that I am a terrible person, right? She said.

It was difficult to take that all again and again. The gap between her calls was short. It was just 15-20 minutes, and getting hit like that was hard for me. I just didn't have the energy to do anything. I cut the call, kept my phone silent, and I slept.

Do you know the feeling of draining yourself to keep the relationship alive? I didn't want to leave the relationship, start a new life, and find someone else. I CONVINCED MYSELF SHE WOULD BE FINE because I didn't want to give up on her. Someday she will understand my feelings for her and change herself.

CHAPTER 21

She and I worked on the same project and had the same work to do daily. Our login and logout timings were the same, and I used to reach home earlier than she did. Because I used to come in my own vehicle. But still, I used to be awake until she got home. That day also, because she used to feel unsafe, as usual, I waited for her to reach home, and when she texted me that "I reached", I just went to sleep.

The phone rang...I lifted.

What are you doing? Sanjana asked.

I was sleeping. I said.

Oh, then sleep! She said.

No, no, tell me, what is it? I asked.

Nothing. I called just like that. Sanjana said.

Okay. Good night. I said.

I went back to sleep, and after 1anhour, received a call again from her.

What are you doing? She asked.

I didn't say that I slept. I said I was doing nothing.

I thought you slept. Okay, no problem. Go and sleep. Sanjana said and cut the call.

I was like, what would I be doing? Of course, I slept! What else would I be doing? I had a long day at work, was tired, and wanted an undisturbed sleep. Yes, she is an overthinker, with many things running through her mind. I have been with her for 6 months now, and every day this happens. Sometimes she would have a few things to say, and I would compromise on my sleep and listen to whatever she said about her family, career, pain, life and everything about her. It's all about her, her, her! I used to feerestless every day.

****

There was an incident where she had a fight with me. I don't remember what the fight for was, but it was awful. I didn't think anything because I was exhausted from the things happening. I put my phone aside and slept like a dead body who didn't know what was happening around me. I don't know what she felt after the fight, she might be regretting what she did, but she called me almost 130 times, and my phone has a lock so no one can open it. My mom took the phone and saw the number on the screen when she called me continuously.

Hello, I am Abhijeet's mother. What is the need to call that many times? My mom asked.

There is a submission that he needs to be done in the office portal. That is the reason I am calling him Aunty. Sanjana said.

He is asleep, and he is tired. Don't call him again; let him sleep, and when he wakes up, I will ensure he knows you called. My mom said.

Sorry, I called only to tell him that. Sanjana said.

This is not his office hours, and if it is that important that it would disturb his peace of mind, then he doesn't need that job. Please don't call him and let him sleep. My mom said.

After that, my mom just cut the call and kept my phone away. Even after this conversation, she called on my phone several times.

I woke up and asked my mom where my phone was. She gave the phone to me and told me what happened when I was asleep.

I called her and asked, why did you call me?

I need to submit the broadband bill. Today is the last day, and I don't know how to do it, so I called you to do that for me. She said.

I remember it, I thought I would do it after getting up, and FYI, re there's 2 days to do that. I said.

Yeah. Please do it; I am not rich like you; I need that money. Sanjana said.

This is what you wanted to say? I asked her.

Yes. she said and cut the call.

I felt miserable after that. Continuous mistreatment from the person makes you feel low all the time. I was going through that phase. I never complained about this. I always tried to explain how it felt, but it continued. It never stopped. I thought that she was a narcissist. I was always patient. But how long can we be patient? It has to break some or the other day. It was literally breaking. But I never decided to leave her side. I was always there in everything, supporting her every decision. My patience was lapsing. It didn't have an expiry date, but it was hard for me to keep myself together. I decided that I needed a break and to travel to energize myself. I asked Satya, one of my college friends, if you want to accompany me. He was leaving for England for higher studies, so he said yes because he wanted to go on a bike ride, like a long road trip. So we decided that we would leave on September 8, 2021. I told her that I needed a break and this would re-energize me.

We started for Coorg on that day, and we reached Chikmagalur on the same day, but it took 12 hours, and on the way, I met with a minor accident. It could have been a major one, but I was wearing all the riding gear, so I survived the impact. If I didn't have the biking gear, my kneecap would have been broken into pieces, and I would not be able to walk appropriately my entire life. That could have been so bad.

The bike was slightly damaged, and the chain and the sprocket were broken. We had to tow the vehicle and finally reached the homestay we booked at 12:00 AM; it took almost 2 hours to travel 10 km. We were so tired, but it was okay. I washed my wounds, and first aid was done after reaching the homestay. I was in pain till then, but the fight or flight hormone didn't make me feel the pain. We repaired the vehicle in the morning and finally went to Mullayanagiri Peak. On the way, I received a call from her.

How are you? Sanjana asked.

I have had a few injuries, but I am fine now. I said. (I messaged her that I met with an accident)

Oh okay! She said.

How are you? I asked.

What will happen to me? I am fine as always. You have to take responsibility for whatever you do. This all-sudden care doesn't matter. She said.

What? Sudden care? I said.

Yes, you went there, to that place, whatever it is, I don't remember the name. You left me and went, right? She said.

You could have come with me if you wanted to. I said.

No, you went to forget me, so go ahead, ignore me. She said.

I was speechless. I didn't know what to say. I kept my mouth shut.

Why did I even call you? It's all a waste of time. Goodbye! She said.

I was devastated after she said that. Am I not understanding her emotions? Am I hurting her that much? You might think she is frustrated that she could not come with me, so she felt that and might have said that. But no, it did not sound like that. It sounded like she hated me more than she loved me.

I didn't cry because I was not alone but with one of my friends. I didn't even let my friend know that I was depressed because that would create disrespect for her in his mind. Because she was doing such things which can be exceedingly hurtful to others. And I might look like I am emotionally weak and unable to handle these things. But these things are tough to handle. I just started to ride after calming myself, and I was at peace taking those twists and turns in the ghats. I was happy that day and didn't respond to calls or messages. We enjoyed ourselves, and we were concentrating on finishing the trip and nothing else. That day after returning, we bought some whiskey, sat out, and drank.

****

Satya saw a girl at the homestay whom he liked immensely and wanted to talk to her. She was accompanied by her friend. Her friend was also beautiful.

Let's go and ask them if they want to have some whiskey. Satya said.

I am not sure, man. I don't have the guts to do that. I said.

Huh…! You are good at flirting and don't have the guts to do that? You are a lord of mischievous and flirting. Come on, man, go and ask at least for me. Satya said.

I tried a couple of times but didn't want to do it, so I failed. If you don't have the will to do it, then the charm doesn't work. That's what happened.

So Satya wrote a beautiful poem on the tissue with my number and Instagram ID and pushed the tissue from the bottom of the door into their room. We just waited, and there was no response at all. We thought they had just slept, so we slept after 1 o'clock at midnight.

We had to start and continue riding the next day, so we didn't know if they got the poem we wrote. We tried to talk to them, but they were busy packing up their stuff, and we were busy, too, because we were already late and had to start early. We thought they didn't get it, and we started.

Satya was ready to stay back for them because he wanted to spend more time at that place, as we could not explore it because of my accident. The worst part was it was raining, and we saw the clouds clearing when we were leaving. We were like, damn!

Hi! I am Neha. (I received a text from her at 12 o'clock in the afternoon, and I didn't check it).

We went half the way, and then I opened and saw the message. I was again like, damn!

I told Satya, and he took a gap and said, "Saale tu pura mood kharab kardiya" (You have spoiled my mood).

I took a deep breath because I thought he would just hit me. Still, he just said that, and I was thankful that "Road pe sabke samne mera beizatti toh nahi hua" (At least he did not hit me on the road in front of everyone).

We had our lunch around 4 o'clock, and we were calling Neha continuously because we were still ready to return with a couple of bottles of wine and surprise them. She didn't pick up the call. We waited almost 3 hours there, and it was already 7 o'clock in the evening. We left that place, and we were on the way. We received a call from Neha around 7:30 PM.

First, he received a call because the last call to her went from his phone. He couldn't pick up because he was obviously riding, and then I started to get a call. Then he signalled that she called and you might be getting a call, and I picked it up because I had the helmet intercom.

Hi Neha, I said with a sweet voice.

Hi Abhijeet! She said with a welcoming voice.

Awww….such a sweet voice. I might have to go to a rehabilitation centre now. I said.

Haha! Why? Neha asked.

Your voice sounds so addicting. I said.

Oh my god! Neha said.

Hahaha! Your smile is what I see now.

Look at the road, Abhijeet. Neha said.

How can I look at the road when you are what I have in my eyes? I said.

God! Now I know how you write these lines. Neha said.

Hahaha! How was it? I asked.

Why do you think I messaged you in the first place? Neha said.

Hahaha! Understood! I said.

I thought you didn't get the tissue, so we left, else we were planning to stay back. I said.

For what? Neha asked.

You know we wanted to talk to you, and we wanted to enjoy your company. If you say, we can ride back to the place. It's not a big task for us to ride back for such a beautiful one. I said.

Oh god! You are flirting like anything. Where did you learn this from? Neha asked.

I am a descendant of Lord Krishna, so I don't need to learn. I got it by birth. I said.

Hahaha! Nice one. A handsome guy like you doesn't need skills in flirting, but it's good that you have it. Anyway, we are leaving tomorrow, so we won't have much time to spend, so you continue the ride, and we will meet when you come to Bangalore. Neha said.

Oh! You are from Bangalore. I said.

Haan, Vaise Bangalore utna durr nahi hai Abhijeet ji! Neha said, (It was basically a dialogue from a movie called M.S. Dhoni).

Hahahaha! Yeah, I stay in Hyderabad, so it's not that far. I said.

Hahaha! She laughed out loud.

What about your friend? Did she read that one? I asked.

She read it and found it interesting, and you look more decent than your friend, whoever it is. She said.

Oh! Why? I asked.

I don't know. I didn't find him attractive. He was more suspicious. Neha said.

Hahaha! My friend was actually interested in her. I said.

Oh! She is getting married next month, so we planned this trip. Neha said.

Unlucky satya. I said.

Hahaha! She laughed out loud again.

We wanted to come back, but you didn't lift the call. I said.

Yar, what happened is my phone battery was dead. I had to leave my phone at a general store, the aunty at the store put it on charge, and we went to Hebbe Falls, then and you know we were drenched in rain while we were going. It rained for a bit only, and then the skies were clear. We were so tired, and our clothes were wet, so I thought I would call you back after returning to the room. Neha said.

Makes sense. No problem, yar, iss bahane. I will get another chance to meet you. I said.

Hahaha! You mischievous person. No problem. You reach and call me, and we will talk. I want you to be safe, so ride safe. Because if something happens to you I would miss all the fun talking to you. I will freshen up a bit. Neha said.

Okay, Neha, Bye! I said with a sweet voice.

Bye, Abhijeet Ji!

She cut the call, and I didn't stop riding because it was getting dark. I said to Satya that we would stop after 100 km and I would tell you what happened. It was great talking to her. We became good friends after that, and I flirted with her once in a while, and she used to speak to me as a friend, and I did too. But it was more like having a person to talk to and nothing else.

CHAPTER 22

I completed my trip and came back. As soon as I returned, I felt I had returned to jail. I didn't feel that freedom, and I didn't feel great to get back. It was tiring to meet Sanjana because she didn't care what I felt. She is always filled with herself, and the conversations with her are all about herself. I didn't feel like I went on a trip. It mostly felt that I was in her glance all the time.

Our office was open. The Covid-19 effect was not that much, so we had to report back to our offices. That day I went to the office, and she was coming to meet me, and our office had a nice place to sit outside. As soon as she saw me, she waved at me.

Hi! I am happy, I am meeting you after so long. Sanjana said.

Me too, I said.

I bought a few things for my baby girl (Her cousin's daughter, who is 7 years old, treats her like her own daughter). She was so happy. Looking at her, I was happy too. Sanjana said.

Yeah. It is great to hear. I said.

Why do you sound like you are not interested in listening? She said.

No, nothing like that. I said.

It is like that. Why do you want to hear me out? You might be busy with your friend. She said.

Who? I asked.

You met someone on your trip, right! She said.

Oh! Neha? I said.

Yes, whatever her name is. She said.

No, no, she is busy these days. I said.

Oh, you know that she is busy. Those conversations are going to that level, right! She said.

What do you want me to say, that I am some kind of playboy? I asked.

You may be, who checks your phone. I don't know. Sanjana said.

You don't trust me? I asked.

No. Sanjana said.

My anger was at its peak, and I just kept quiet. I was not speaking.

What is the use of speaking to you? You just keep spoiling the mood. I will just go and work. She said.

I kept quiet. Sanjana got up and walked away and didn't turn back. I felt bad. Very bad. She might be jealous of what was happening, but it was not so deep. Neha is my friend. She had a boyfriend, and I have a girlfriend. I met her in 2021, and it's 2023 now. I went to Bangalore once, but I didn't even meet her. What we just did was talk and joke around. But she never understood, or I should say she never trusted me.

CHAPTER 23

Trust but verify. Don't trust blindly; You never know the intentions behind that cute face - A.R. Murthy.

Abhijeet, can I tell you something? Sanjana said.

Yeah sure! I said.

I kissed my Best Friend once. She said.

Was it after meeting me or before meeting me? I asked.

It was before you. She said.

Yeah! Then it's okay. I don't care about your past. I said.

But if I say that, I still feel like kissing him then. She said.

What? I asked.

Yeah, not only my best friend; when I look at some other guys as well, I feel different. She said.

Different in what sense? I asked.

Different in the sense that I want to have sex with them. Sanjana said.

What do you mean by saying that? I said.

Why are you overreacting? She asked.

I am not overreacting. I mean, what else do you want me to do? Support you in this? I said.

You always behave like this. You keep judging me all the time. Sanjana said.

If this is how it is, then I am done. I said.

Oh, then, I am, too; you can date Neha or someone else. It's not new for you to date multiple girls simultaneously. She said.

What are you saying? I was never disloyal to you, and you know everything about my past, and I would never do something like that to anyone in my life. I said.

Who knows, you might have just lied to me. Sanjana said.

If you want to trust me or not, it's ultimately your decision, and looking at your cognitive abilities, you don't have such a capacity to think of someone good. I doubt you will ever be able to do that. I said.

Oh, now you are making fun of me and insulting me. Who knows, that phone of yours has so many stories. Sanjana said.

Oh, you want to take a look at it, then take a look at it. I don't delete messages like you do. I said.

She actually took my phone and started reading Neha's chat. I remembered that we had conversations where I was telling her about what Sanjana was doing with me, and, of course, some jokes that she and I did. I was still okay because I thought she should read it. Still, I was feeling very uncomfortable that she would make a mess out of it again, and she would be showing that as a reason to break up with me. I know she was not good enough for me, and breaking up with her is better. Still, she would say the same thing to others, that I am a playboy and pervert who is behind all girls, and I did not want the past to repeat itself. I didn't like the same things to happen which happened with my first relationship and which I mentioned about it at the beginning. I took away my phone and deleted the whole conversation with Neha. She confirmed that I was cheating on her, and we were in a cafe where so many people were, and she created a mess there. She even made me call Neha and spoke to her very badly, which is why she is not on good terms with me. She talks to me but not like before. I cried like anything that day, and she didn't even care. She went from that place, and I was sitting there only and calling her. Then she came back and asked me if we were breaking up. I said I don't want to. Then she talked like nothing happened and returned to saying all her problems. I felt I was with some Psychopath. She wants someone to listen to her, and no one does that except me. She again said that I wanted to leave because she was getting late. We both went out of the cafe. She gave me a nasty look, and I was still with a sad face, and the look was clearly saying that I didn't care whatever you felt right now.

I felt terrible and called Neha on my way; I obviously had my intercom on and apologized to her. I cried when talking to her, but it didn't matter anymore.

There were hundreds of fights every day, and now I feel like why I was holding onto the relationship when it was not working out.

How much effort you put in, it just doesn't matter. At the end of the day, you just keep explaining yourself too much, and it becomes a bad habit of making yourself low. You lose the spark in you, and the effort just takes a lot of things from you. It just doesn't drain your energy. It takes your self-respect, self-esteem and every fucking thing used to make you feel better before. Being nice costs you everything. Maybe that is why the world we are in right now is bizarre and wicked in its own way. You don't know whom to trust and whom to keep around you. It just doesn't feel safe anymore.

Love and relationships are two different things. You can love someone and not be in a relationship with them, but you can not be in a relationship without loving them. - Ritvik Gadhey.

I started to overthink and was not able to keep my emotions in control. I felt like a volcano that was ready to burst. It was winter, and I could not sleep sometimes at night because I could not think straight, and my mind just didn't stop thinking. I just used to go to my bathroom and keep the tap on, and I used to keep my head under the water that came out from the tap, and I don't know if it was because the water used to be cold; I would be coming back to my senses. I started to overeat and gained a lot of weight than I was, and I wasted all my salary by just sitting at home and doing nothing apart from eating.

She stopped talking to me. Then my birthday came, and I didn't want that to be celebrated because I was obviously in depression, and it was at its peak.

Let's plan something for his birthday. Sanjay said (My office colleague).

What can we plan? We have work that day, and I don't know if we can get leave. If we get to leave, then we can go to some pub to chill. Spoorthy said.

We will ask the lead. Maybe he will approve for us. Abhijeet will get leave anyway because special occasion leave doesn't need prior approval. Sanjay said.

He will get leave, but we will not get one that day. Spoorthy said.

Let's ask and check. Sanjay said.

Fortunately, they did not get leave that day, and they just planned a cake cutting. It was great, and it was so nice of them that they had planned it. I was happy, or I must say they made me feel happy. Sanjana was present, but I could sense her absence. She just spoke the way she always used to, and I found it annoying on my birthday. She then left to meet her best friend. By then, I got used to her behaviour and was okay. We went to the cafeteria to have our dinner.

We ordered chicken fried rice and chicken noodles. We were having our food, and Sanjana came and had a couple of spoons. I don't remember what she said, but it spoiled our mood.

Does she do this all the time? Sanjay said.

No, it just happens sometimes. Let's ignore that. I said.

But it was clearly evident that she meant it in a bad way. Sanjay gave me a look which clearly said, "Dude! Why are you still together?"

Whenever I think of leaving her and say enough is enough. Let's break up. She used to use her emotional crying face and behave as if she was devastated I don't know how true it is, but she used it as one elder wand. Her narcissistic traits are evident. All the fucking time, she changes the situation in a perfect way that I was the one who made a mistake, and there is no one to blame but only me.

CHAPTER 24

*H*er best friend, who used to manipulate her in such a way, or she wanted him to control her, I don't know what it was, but I was the one who suffered the most.

Why don't you tell him you are in a relationship with me? I said.

He will not understand, and he will break the friendship with me. Sanjana said.

If he breaks the friendship, then let it be; why do you need that toxic friendship? Who doesn't even understand that you have moved on and with me now? I said. (She actually had a crush on him before).

Why don't you understand my feelings? He will not understand, and he will be behind me. She said.

You want to keep the friendship, no matter how much it will affect our relationship. Right? I said.

Even though I explain, you will not understand. Sanjana said.

Oh! You explain too? When did this happen? I am the one who explains it to you all the time. I said.

Her self-centred behaviour was always on, and I have explained to her so much all the time that these are a few things that require your effort to keep the relationship alive, but she never understood my point. Maybe explaining things has become my habit, and I still do that often. It happens unintentionally, and I explain too much, making me sound annoying and boring to others.

Every time you do this. Sanjana said and cut the phone off. She even switched it off, and I clearly, as usual, didn't know what I did.

****

After some time, she called me and asked if I could talk to his best friend because she said she was in a relationship. He did not understand, and he proposed to her.

Yeah, it looks creepy, but he did that.

"What will I talk about? When he proposed to you, what did you say? I asked.

Nothing I kept quiet. Sanjana said.

I found it very bad, and it was evident that she was not even ready to defend herself from him. There was an instance where she told me he wouldn't understand her, but I was the one who understood her and supported her all the time. That is the reason I am different from him, and I am special to her. But I don't know where that feeling for me flew off.

Okay. I will talk to him. I said.

She sent his number, and I messaged him on WhatsApp.

Hi! I am Abhijeet. I am Sanjana's Boyfriend. She tried to say she was in a relationship with me, and you wouldn't understand. What is the problem? I texted.

I didn't get a reply for a long time, and then he finally replied.

"I don't know who the fuck you are, but why are you even with her when you are such a 'pervert' and an awful person. I don't want to see you with her; I love her, and will not be good to you. Don't even try to message me, and never dare call me. I am not interested in talking to you." He replied.

That one word, pervert, where did this come from. I confronted her about this and asked her why he said this to me?

I don't know. She replied.

He is not some random person; he is your best friend. He had the audacity to say that to me, and it is clearly your negligence that he said that to me. What did you say about me to him? I asked.

Yes, I said, you are a pervert and rapist. She replied.

What? I replied.

You are the same as my cousin; all are the same. What you all men want is the vagina of a girl to fuck her. All the men out there are perverts and rapists. She said.

I clearly know where this is going. Just say to me, "Have you said something to him like that?" I asked.

When he was not talking to me about the fact that I am in a relationship with you, "I just said that you are a pervert. I don't want to be in a relationship with him." She said.

And why did you say this? I asked.

Because he will start talking to me. Sanjana said.

I threw the phone away with that single message. All the bad things that happened in my past were still haunting me, and I heard something like this from her, and I was totally fucked up and broken by what she said.

She called me as I was not replying to her, and my phone was still okay, so I picked up the phone.

Sorry. Sanjana said.

I cut the call because I was crying like hell. She was calling me continuously, and I had to pick up the phone.

My trust and my love for you is gone. I said.

No, please. I want to be with you. Sanjana said.

If you want me, you must earn my trust and love again. I will only get back to you if you do that. This is the final decision I am taking. Yes, I loved and still want you, but I will not give in, just like I always do, but you have to earn me. I said and cut the call.

After that, she tried to get back to me by manipulating her way into me. But I didn't let her manipulate me this time. After a few days, I didn't get her calls anymore; when I asked Spoorthy what she told about me?

You were such a pain in her ass. That's why she left you. Spoorthy said.

I was like, Haha! Yeah, I was the pain in her ass. I cried a lot, and it physically and mentally showed a lot of effect on me. History always repeats itself. I heard the same things that I heard when I broke up with my first love, and it happened the same. I left the company and was so broken; it affected me so much that I could not look at any girl with lust or just feel for any girl. It was tough for me. I sometimes feel that I am an Asexual species or that I don't feel for any girl. The feelings are just dead. But I should say that I had slept peacefully, not every night, but at least when I slept, I was so free that I didn't have the pressure in my mind that I had when I was with her.

Sometimes when things seem to be going wrong, they are going right for reasons you are yet to understand." — Alan Cohen

It was difficult to move on, but I have accepted that no matter what you do, the people who are not meant to be with you, however you try, won't stay in your life. God sometimes sends you the signals that she or he is not meant for you, but we ignore those because we feel that everything will be fine over time. But they don't. And when you ignore those signals sent by God, you will be taught a more significant lesson that will break you from in and out. I have often overlooked the signs, and they destroyed every bit of me.

CHAPTER 25

"Hope is being able to see that there is light despite all the darkness" - Desmond Tutu.

I have always believed that there will be hope. Whenever I suffer, I have always stayed with the hope that things will get better and I will never have to get to the part where I don't have to let her go. I have waited very patiently where I can have one more walk, one more breakfast, one more date, one more dinner and one more night. When we add up this one more, it will be equal to a whole life. But reality will hit us so severely that all our hopes will be lost. When I met her, everything was new and exciting; the possibilities seemed endless. I had hoped and put my every drop of sweat to keep this relationship alive. I think it never worked out how I wanted it to, and I still don't blame her for what she did. Because there were instances where I did not reach her expectations. Where I could have avoided a few fights, I did fight with her. But I have always fought for us, which she didn't believe in. Things have now passed, and she has become my past. I can't do anything about it right now, and I could just hope for my happiness.

****

Unfortunately, sometimes, when things like this happen, when life gives up on you, everything breaks in and out. When something breaks, if the pieces are large enough, you can fix it. But things just don't break; they shatter.

When someone loves you back, they don't love you. They just love the fact that you are giving them affection and attention. This later definitely changes, and they just don't love you because you are giving them this and that. But if it does not change and you still love them, you will be taken for granted, and they don't think twice about throwing you in the garbage when you are not needed any more. When I told Sanjana that I was leaving you and this was over, it felt more like she left me rather than me leaving her. When I asked her to earn me over again, she didn't even try to do anything to get me back. She just left me then and there. I was a fool who initially thought I was speaking for myself and felt proud, but a fool who didn't realize that I was talking for myself with the wrong person. For the next two months, I just lied down and did nothing. Then I was like, enough is enough, and I joined the gym again. (I have been working out since 2019 but could not focus on it due to CoVid-19 and the stress that I had from my job). I have tried to change things and went to the gym every day and found a new job, a better one. Tried to learn something new and focus on my future. Everything seemed real, but nothing was like before.

I used to make everyone laugh, but I showed my fake smile. It was not me. I felt like someone had control over me. I overthink every time and decide to not share what I am going through. If I share my pain, it doesn't decrease; it increases more. I know I wanted a shoulder to cry on, but nothing would ever make sense if I kept finding a shoulder. I will keep making the same mistake that I always did. Looking for acceptance from others, this is what most people do. I kept things to myself and healed from within. I started to look at the bigger picture and understood the difference between love and a relationship.

You know, Love is eternal, and relationships are not. Love is energy; as the famous physics law says, energy can neither be destroyed nor created. It is present in this universe. But in a relationship, it always needs fuel for its survival. You need to pour in your efforts, commitments and love from both individuals. You can love someone and not be in a relationship with them, but you have to have love if you are in a relationship. If that is not there, keeping the relationship alive is tough.

This is for everyone out there. If you don't love him/her. Don't tell them that you love them and then leave. There might be situations where you feel that things are not working out. If both think that, sit, talk things out, and leave. That will be mutual. But if you are dry and then leave, it just makes him/her feel that no one loves them in this world. They become heartless and do stupid things. They start to say they are the only ones in this world but keep craving a person who will listen to, understand, and love them. Don't hurt people!

I kept trying and kept pushing myself. It never felt the same. I was breaking every day. I was strong enough, which kept me alive, or else I would have been a victim of suicide. I have always had a broken heart and always looked for love. I always craved love. I have seen a reel on Instagram where it said that love is a kind of drug. It can lead to addiction. I think that is what happened to me. When you are in love, this rush of chemicals releases in your brain. The dopamine levels will be at their peak. Love will secrete the same level of dopamine that releases when you take cocaine and nicotine. Love is not just an emotion. It's a drug which makes you crave it.

I had a broken heart when Riya left me, and I always wanted someone to love me. I kept loving people, relationship after relationship. I was not using them; I wanted love; I wanted to escape the reality of the broken heart. Though I got over Riya, I could not get over the love I was in when she left. That is when I started to ruin my life. I got into a relationship with Radha because I wanted someone. But when I had to leave her, I felt empty again. I didn't want that to happen when I was with Sanjana; that is why I didn't care how much I was in pain; I just ignored the fact that I was suffering in the relationship. I wanted the person to stay, so I have been bearing her much more than a person with self-respect should. People often misunderstood me when I entered a relationship with multiple people, not at once but one after the other. It was not because I was a playboy but because I craved love. This romantic love phenomenon makes people do unimaginable things. When I was bearing her, I was too scared to jump out of that relationship because I felt I would never get that love again. I didn't want to give up on the fact that I loved her so much. But I did not realize that when you are scared to do something that restricts you from doing what you want, that is when you need to do it, and that gives you the satisfaction of achieving it. I was unable to do it because I was scared.

I have not got into any relationship; I have shut myself down for love and any kind of relationship. I started to grow and heal in silence. I should repair myself. If I am the one who is spoiled and starts to bring someone into my life, there is always a probability that I will spoil their life as well. I opened the windows of my brain and shut the door to let all the negativity pass from the ventilation and did not let anything in. I started to excel in my job and Started to do photography which I learned during my college. Earned recognition and did everything I could. Things were going well, not great as I expected but good in their way. I started to travel alone and learn the way of life. Thankfully, my new job was remote. I have been travelling from place to place for the last 6 months, meeting different people and gaining new experiences.

CHAPTER 26

*M*eanwhile, I met this great woman at my office; it was a remote job, but we were connected through WhatsApp. I started to realize that she could be the one, but as I said, I had closed the door to my heart, so I was not ready to let her in. We started to talk daily, and I began to get to know her better. I am a fool. My understanding levels are insignificant, but she often understood me though I misinterpreted her. After such a thing, who would not get a feeling for a woman? I mean, what does a man need? Especially a person like me who overthinks things that are not even needed. She started to understand that I was in pain, and even when I misinterpreted her, she made me feel special by just talking nicely.

I was still traveling, as my job allowed me to work remotely; I have been visiting new places and meeting new people daily. By this time, I have learned that this kind of thing keeps happening, and I have moved on entirely and with no baggage of despair. Even the glimpses of it were still present; I mean, who wouldn't have that. I have met so many people, and everybody had their stories. Everyone had a past that hurt them, and I have not seen a man or a woman happy. They had the most brutal breakups and goodbyes. We feel people are heartless, but deep down, they have this beautiful soul in them that they keep striving for a person to be with them.

Love is the most powerful feeling in this world; people do crazy things for it. I have seen men and women who left everything they had and were travelling and living. Some try to forget, and some try to celebrate that they are in love. The kind of things that you get to know while travelling are the ultimate in your life.

I met Aahana twice, and there is a sense of realization that I want her. I never opened up myself, but I really wanted to. I didn't realize I loved her because I knew she wouldn't want that. She has faced a lot of things, and she couldn't allow something like that to happen to her again, and I never forced this on her. The decision was always hers to take. I was in Shimla, and I realized for the first time that I love her. I tried to put forth my feelings, but things are complicated, right? I don't know; maybe I think that way. She doesn't want me, and I am okay with that so much that I can keep my feelings for her to myself and still see her cherish. I am a broken piece of glass… huh, huh….nah! I am glass that shattered utterly, but she is the light that makes me glitter. SHE CAN MAKE ME FEEL AT PEACE when I let her into my life.

Ye mat sochna ki, ye pagal toh nahi hogaya? (Don't think that I lost my mind) Haha! Yes, it's weird, right. I know that she is not in my life as my girlfriend or wife. But I want her to be mine.

She has a passion for singing, and the songs that I heard from her are songs that I will never forget. The moment I sit alone in a cafe, I don't feel that I am sitting alone. She would stand at that mic and sing on the stage while I enjoyed listening to her. Whenever I miss her, I close my eyes and remember our conversations, and I feel she is sitting with me and talking to me. I know this is not reality, yes it is not, but even in her absence, I feel like smiling, and the memories of her just keep passing in front of my eyes.

Love is mysterious in its own way. The strength that one-sided love has is unbeatable. As I said, love is eternal; you can love someone and not be in a relationship with them. I have started loving her so intensely that it doesn't make me feel alone anymore.

You know what? She says that she keeps nagging. Yes, she does, and I listen to everything patiently, and she has called me stupid for that. Yes, I am stupid! When she talks, it is not tiring to listen at all. It makes me feel alive. Survival was very much hard for me, but when I am with her over call, I feel the breath that I take in. I feel of the blood in my veins that my heart pumps in and every electrical impulse my brain produces. Is she some drug? No. It would be a lie to say that I love her more than myself. If I say she is the most desirable for me, it's a lie because she is not just a thing I can get when I want and forget later.

She is a person that I will always wish for, and I hope that I will love her forever without forgetting the value of her presence.

****

I was travelling to Spiti alone on a bike. I have covered almost 1000 km, and on every curve I took, I have always remembered her. I know precisely why it is happening to me. I find peace in the mountains; when I look at those mountains, I see her because she is that peace I wanted. I rest at ease when she is around. You might have this question: I have met her only twice, and how do I find peace around her? It is not important for the person to always be around. It is our feeling for that person when they are not around us. That is enough.

I am the most egoistic person. But her words make the ego disappear, and that cute face, Ab kya hi bolum! (What else can I say now!)

I have rode to the highest post office in the world, the Hikkim post office. I wanted to post a Postcard to her with a beautiful picture on it. I wrote what I felt at the back of it but didn't post it because I didn't want her to think I was trying to force her to feel for me. It should happen by itself, and I could just wait for that. I made sure that she knew that I loved her, and it was now for her to decide if she would want me in her life, and I knew she was very aspirational. Probably I am too. I aspire to get her in life so much that I can wait for her until the end of life. I have always told her I could pray and wish for her, but I can't force her to be mine. She said that I would get hurt in the end, but my love for her never went away and will never go, maybe. This sounds very foolish, right? It sounds like I am returning to the addiction of having love in my life. I assure you that this differs from the romantic love phenomenon I was discussing. I am not craving love, I am feeling it right now, and I have not been in a relationship for a year and a half. Probably I will never get into a relationship if that's not her. I have made myself strong first and then opened my heart to let Aahana in.

I have decided not to post it. It was winding heavily at Hikkim. I always treated the mountains as gods, and I closed my eyes and made a wish, "Dear mountains, you have the power to change anything. Change my fate and make her mine. As I said, I can just wish for her. I will wish for her ever and forever.

CHAPTER 27

My dear Aahana, It has been 9 months since our friendship started. We have spoken for maybe 100 hours, laughed 1000 times, and discussed many things. I have never felt something like this for you. You were definitely a special one for me, but I didn't have the feeling of having you in my life. But, I have now, which reminds me of you every time. Whenever I miss you, I close my eyes and think of you, and it reminds me of your smell, touch and the smile on that beautiful face.

Mai jaha bhi dekhu tum hi jo dikhti ho,

Ab Kaise bhula du tujhe,

Aankhe kholta hu toh fursat nahi milti hai,

Aur jab aankhe band karum toh, Tera chehra samne aata hai,

Jab tum hi ho khayalo mai, toh kya hi hai mera qasoor?

Yes, I love you, and I want to hear the same from you. But I can't force you to say it. I wish that you would be mine, and there is nothing I would want in my life apart from getting you. When you are around me, what I do makes me grow as a new person every day. You have the magic in you that lights up my soul. Maybe it's not your speciality; perhaps the feeling I have for you makes me think refreshingly. Just having your presence in my thoughts makes me feel great. Maybe that's why I have filled you in every inch of my soul. That may be why if you don't want to have me in your life, I will still be okay because you are what I have in me. The energy that I get from remembering will make me achieve anything. It's very cool here, and I don't have anything to keep me warm except for the leather jacket that we bought when I was in Delhi. I will bear this weather because these mountains have made me realize that you are the one with whom I can share my life. But you might hurt me if you don't want me. So, I am leaving this feeling to the mountains. These mountains made me realize that you are the one for me, and these mountains will decide if I will ever have you in my life.

CHAPTER
28

This was the Postcard that I wanted to send to her Ritvik. Abhijeet said.

Wow! I said, looking at the picture and what he wrote at the back of it.

But I didn't send this to her because she doesn't want me right now, and I don't want to force her. Abhijeet said.

I really understand, I said.

When I started to tell this story, it was all about me, but when I ended it, it was about her, my Aahana. He said.

"My Aahana", you said, right? But she is still not yours. I said.

Yes, but it doesn't mean I have rights on her. When I say 'My Aahana', it means my feelings for her. She is the inspiration that I have in my life. I don't know what she has done, but I have a story to tell because of her. He said.

Great! I said.

She says Choosing her is stupidity, but I would choose her whatever the result. And I wish that she chooses me as I chose her. I sometimes wonder if God might have written my destiny already, then why there is a need to wish. Maybe God has written

"As you wish!" for the part of my life with her. If I wish for her with my whole heart, then I might get her.

Aahana, her name, means Ray of sunlight. I am the shattered pieces of glass. When she is with me, I will shine like a diamond. He said.

****

Can I get a glass of water, please? I said.

Sure sir. The air hostess said.

The air hostess gets a glass of water.

Here's the water, sir. She said.

No, the water is not for me. It's for this gentleman. I said.

Okay. Please take it, sir. She said and gave me a different kind of look.

Thank you. I said anyway.

You're welcome, sir. She said and left.

Have it; this will calm you down a bit. I said.

Abhijeet had water and kept down the glass.

Thanks, Ritvik. He said.

Don't mention it. Are you okay now? I asked.

Yes, I am okay now. Abhijeet said.

You love her so much, one-sided love, right! Is it easy for you to love someone without expecting it in return? I asked.

It is not easy, Ritvik, not at all! He said.

Then why are you still loving her? Don't you feel the pain? I asked.

I said, it is not easy, but it's not painful either. It's the most beautiful feeling you will ever have. He said.

How? I asked.

Because when you love someone, you don't just love them; you love their freedom to make a choice. If they don't love you back, then it doesn't mean you have to stop loving them. If you stop, then it is not love. Love is like an energy; it can neither be created nor destroyed. If you stop loving, then you are ending it. If you were able to end it, then that was never love. You know, people don't understand what love is. He said.

Then what is love? I asked.

Love is giving even when you know that you might never get it. He said.

Hmm...! I sighed.

****

When you look at my story, I never stopped loving the other 3 with whom I was in a relationship. I might have let them go but I never gave up the feeling. When Riya and I broke up, I knew she cheated on me, and I could have tried to destroy her. The cruelty was present in me. But I let her go thinking that she would be happy.

When I broke up with Radha, I thought of her well-being and gave up on her, but I have always suffered and felt for her.

When I broke up with Sanjana, it was painful as hell, but then I understood that that's what she wanted, and I was no good for her. I never blamed Sanjana for anything. He said.

I understand. I said.

And now, I love Aahana more than I ever imagined, and I will never give up on her. I will always love her, whether she is with me or not. He said.

I have never met a person like you in my life. You're crazy. I said.

Haha! Indeed I am. He said.

But I really wish that you get Aahana. I said.

I hope so too! He said.

People don't understand the value of love these days, but you know it very well. If Aahana gets you, she will be lucky. I said.

Haha! I will be too. He said.

Kind attention to the passengers; we have arrived at the destination. We request all the passengers to brace themselves and be ready. We are soon going to land at the Rajiv Gandhi international airport.

Seat belt, please! Air hostess said.

Okay! Abhijeet and I said.

Dear Passengers, Air India welcomes you to Rajiv Gandhi International Airport, Hyderabad. You may now get off the flight. Thank you for flying with us.

Yar, I hate goodbyes! I said.

Haha! I don't hate it, so goodbye! He said.

Dude, shut up! I said.

Haha! He laughed.

I am from Hyderabad, and you are from Hyderabad, and we can meet anytime. I really would like to meet you again. I said.

He smiled and said nothing.

Can you please move forward? The other passenger said.

Oh! Sure, sorry. Abhijeet, you wait at the flight exit. Let me get my stuff. I said.

He nodded and moved towards the exit.

I took the bag and found the Postcard lying on the seat that he had given me while he told his story.

This guy forgot the main thing. I said.

I took it and walked towards the door. I didn't find him waiting there.

Have you seen the man who was sitting beside me? I asked the air hostess.

Yes, sir. He went out. She said.

Thank you! I said.

You're welcome. She said.

I went out, and he was nowhere to be found. I thought he might be at the baggage belt, and I hurried and went to see. I looked everywhere and didn't find him. Then I walked towards the exit, and I didn't find him. I thought he might have gone to the washroom and waited near the baggage belt to see if I could find him there.

Almost 30 minutes passed, and he did not arrive. I wanted to see him, get his contact details, and hand him the Postcard he had left with me. I thought of asking for his details with Air India and reached its help desk.

****

Hey! I need help. I need the contact details of the person who sat with me on the flight. I said.

I am sorry, sir; we are not supposed to share that information, and we do not have access to that information. The man who sat at the help desk said.

He forgot a Postcard that is with me. This is a very important Postcard that he needs to have. This needs to reach him. I don't know where he went, and I need his details. I said.

I am sorry, sir; the information is confidential, and we will not be able to share the information. Besides, it is just a matter of a picture. We will not be able to help you. He said.

Just shut up! How can you say such a bizarre thing? You are here to help a customer, not to pass some comment. How would you know the importance of this. I shouted at him.

Is there any problem, sir; the manager came and said.

Yes, there is a problem. This guy here has just downgraded the value of an important thing. I said.

We are sorry, sir; We can't help you with the contact details, but we can check and let the person know it is with you. We will dial his number and inform him of this. The manager said.

Yes, please do. I said.

The manager opened the system and asked me for the seat and flight numbers.

My seat number is 16B, my seat number is 16C, and my flight number is AI - 542. I said.

Thank you, sir. He said.

He checked it several times and asked me, "Can you please confirm the name of the person beside you?"

His name is Abhijeet. I said.

Okay. He said.

Is there a problem? I asked.

Sir, the passenger's name matches the seat and flight numbers, but....

But what? I asked.

But, sir, the passenger you are talking about never boarded the flight. He said.

CHAPTER 29

*W*hat? I said in shock.

Yes, sir, the details are correct. He was supposed to fly from Delhi to Hyderabad but never took the flight. The manager said.

There must be a mistake or some glitch. He took the flight, and I had a conversation with him. Please check once again. I said.

Sir, I have reviewed several times, and there is no record of his taking the flight. There is no baggage record. He never came to the airport as well. The manager said.

Can you just dial his number and check? Please do this for me. I said.

He was reluctant too now, but he called him.

Sir, the number is not reachable. He said.

Please check for any alternate number. This is important. I said.

He checked and tried an alternate number. But it was also not reachable.

Sorry, sir; at this point, there is nothing else that we can do. He said.

I understand. I said.

****

I was totally in shock and didn't know what I should do. I sat in a chair in the airport and was just looking at the picture. And it raised a question for me. If the person I met did not take the flight, how did I get this Postcard? How do I know his story?

I closed my eyes and got to thinking. I suddenly remembered what he said.

You see, Ritvik, I have suffered a lot, and I don't know where my fate takes me, but I am ready for it. Abhijeet said.

Don't you blame anyone for what happened to you? I said.

What is the need to blame anyone?

When I broke up with Riya, it taught me the first lesson - "Always believe in yourself, no matter what others say about you."

When I broke up with Radha, it taught me the second lesson - "When you love someone, never let them go and never give up." Letting her go was indeed for her own good, but it meant that I gave up on her.

When I broke up with Sanjana, it was merely karma that I had to suffer for what I had done with Radha. You can even escape death sometimes, but you will never escape the karma for what you did.

Now, I love Aahana, and there is no chance of giving up on her. I would love her until my death. And if she doesn't want me, I will wait until she wants me. If she never wants me, I will grant her wish, and I hold the power of letting her go. But the only regret I would have is, "I told Aahana that I love her, but she doesn't know how much I love her. I will regret that I couldn't explain how much I love her. I'll never say goodbye to anyone. If I ever say that, then I would no longer exist. Abhijeet said.

****

That's it! He said goodbye to me! When we were on the flight. He said he would not exist the day he said goodbye.

I opened my eyes.

But how is it possible? I asked myself.

I know that I will never be able to find an answer to this question. There is a similar incident I went through when I was a kid. I was 8 or 9 years old, and I used to travel on the bus from home to school and vice versa. I was on the bus playing Rubix cube while returning home after school. I realized a bit late that my stop had come. Some students were way older than me and were talking while they were standing exactly at the exit. They were doing foot boarding at the open exit of the bus.

What are your plans, bro? A guy at the exit asked.

As usual, I am going home anyway. I will take a rest and chill out. The mystery guy said.

They continued talking, and the bus stopped at the bay for just 2 or 3 seconds. And as they were occupying the exit wholly, I could not get down, and the bus started to move. I began to cry because I didn't know what to do. I am just 8 years old and don't know any route except the way between my school and home. I don't remember my father's phone number either. The mystery guy took me a little away from the exit and promised to walk me to the same bus bay I get down every day, and from there, I could go home. We got down at the next bus bay, which was almost 3 Km away from the bus bay I usually get down at. He consoled me until I calmed down and took me to the bus bay.

See, I told you right, nothing would happen. We are here, at the place where you get down. He said.

I smiled and hugged him, and said, "Thank you".

Now take care and reach home safely. He said.

Sure, I smiled and nodded.

I called him the mystery guy because he said he would go to his home with his friend. But he mysteriously took the next bus on the other side. I was like, wait, what? He was going home. Now, where is he going?

I shrugged my shoulders!

This incident that happened with Abhijeet is also something like that. Has no meaning how he disappeared. But while leaving, he just gave the hope that "When something bad happens to you, there is also something good that is waiting for you". Life always has to move on. You see, when Abhijeet faced this in his personal life, he always learnt a lesson from it, which always made him better. He looked for himself, constantly changing his life. He got better at it. He might be required to get much better, but he is getting there. Life always allows you to make things better. That is what I learnt from him.

I hope that he gets Aahana if he exists. I know this Postcard was not delivered to her, and she would never know how much he loves her. Maybe that is why fate chose me to meet him to deliver the message to her. It might never reach her because it is with me now, and I don't have her address to post it.

This book proves that the Postcard exists and shows Abhijeet's love for Aahana.

The Postcard that had this picture that Abhijeet could not send to his Aahana

www.ingramcontent.com/pod-product-compliance
Lightning Source LLC
LaVergne TN
LVHW041608070526
838199LV00052B/3033